Careers in Focus

LANDSCAPING AND HOLTICULTURE

Ferguson
An imprint of Infobase Publishing

Careers in Focus: Landscaping and Horticulture

Copyright © 2008 by Infobase Publishing

Ferguson
An imprint of Infobase Publishing
132 West 31st Street
New York NY 10001

Library of Congress Cataloging-in-Publication Data

Careers in focus. Landscaping & horticulture. — 1st ed.
   p. cm.
  Includes bibliographical references and index.
  ISBN-13: 978-0-8160-7280-4 (hardcover: alk. paper)
  ISBN-10: 0-8160-7280-9 (hardcover: alk. paper) 1. Horticulture—Vocational guidance—Juvenile literature. 2. Landscaping industry—Vocational guidance—Juvenile literature. I. J.G. Ferguson Publishing Company. II. Title: Landscaping & horticulture. III. Title: Landscaping and horticulture.
  SB446.38.C37 2008
  635.023—dc22
                        2007040869

Ferguson books are available at special discounts when purchased in bulk quantities for businesses, associations, institutions, or sales promotions. Please call our Special Sales Department in New York at (212) 967-8800 or (800) 322-8755.

You can find Ferguson on the World Wide Web at http://www.fergpubco.com

Text design by David Strelecky
Cover design by Salvatore Luongo

Printed in the United States of America

MP MSRF 10 9 8 7 6 5 4 3 2 1

This book is printed on acid-free paper.

Table of Contents

Introduction

Careers in Focus: Landscaping and Horticulture describes a variety of careers in the landscaping and horticultural industries—in laboratories, nurseries and greenhouses, offices, farm fields, vineyards, golf courses, grasslands and prairies, private backyards, and city parks.

Although job settings vary greatly in landscaping and horticulture, all individuals in this field—whether horticultural therapists using nature to treat people with mental illness, groundskeepers planting begonias to beautify the grounds of a large hotel, landscape architects using computer-aided design technology to create a new city garden, horticulturists striving to create a new fruit hybrid, or horticultural inspectors ensuring that a tomato harvest is safe for your dinner table—share a deep love of nature and the environment.

Careers in landscaping and horticulture offer a great range of earnings potential and educational requirements. Earnings range from minimum wage for horticultural technicians to $200,000 or more for very experienced and successful golf course superintendents and nursery owners and managers. A few of these careers—such as groundskeeper and horticultural technician—require little formal education, but are excellent starting points for a career in the industry. Others, such as enologist, farmer, and nursery owner, require little formal education, but require comprehensive knowledge and experience in the field. Other jobs, such as farm crop production technician, require some postsecondary training. Many positions in the industry (such as agricultural scientist, botanist, golf course superintendent, horticultural therapist, horticulturist, landscape architect, and soil scientist) require a minimum of a bachelor's degree. Advanced degrees—especially for science careers—are usually required for the best positions.

The employment outlook in landscaping and horticulture varies greatly by industry segment, with opportunities in landscaping and horticultural services good and those in agriculture on the decline. The nursery and greenhouse industry is the fastest growing segment of the U.S. agriculture industry, according to the U.S. Department of Agriculture. It is a major provider of jobs and had sales of approximately $16 billion in 2005. Opportunities will be best for arborists, grounds managers, groundskeepers, horticultural technicians, landscape architects, landscapers, and lawn and gardening service owners.

Employment in the agricultural industry is expected to decline through 2014, according to the U.S. Department of Labor. Overproduction, increasing productivity, and industry consolidation have reduced opportunities in the industry—especially for self-employed farmers. The U.S. Department of Labor predicts that several trends should help farmers and other specialized workers in this industry. Some farmers are prospering by focusing on growing specialty crops, participating in farmer-owned and -operated cooperatives, or switching to all-organic farming practices in response to public fears about the effects of pesticides and fertilizers used in traditional agriculture. Another important development in agriculture involves methods of processing grains to make new products and helping farmers to deal with crop surpluses. In many agriculture-based states, adding value to agricultural products is the largest creator of wealth and jobs. The pursuit of new uses for farm crops will provide many jobs for those involved in processing and will also provide farmers with new markets for their crops. For example, corn is used for ethanol, sweeteners, feed products, corn oil, and lactic acid. Studies are underway that will expand corn's uses to include adhesives, paper and packaging, nonprescription medical products, and even plastic.

Food safety is an important issue that will impact jobs for food scientists, horticultural scientists, and inspectors. Recent outbreaks of mad cow disease and foot-and-mouth disease in livestock in Europe have prompted heightened efforts to detect and prevent these problems in the United States. There are also concerns about the West Nile virus, anthrax, and residual pesticides in plant products. Efforts are also being made to protect this industry from agriterrorism.

Each article in this book discusses in detail a particular horticulture-related occupation. The articles in *Careers in Focus: Landscaping and Horticulture* appear in Ferguson's *Encyclopedia of Careers and Vocational Guidance*, but have been updated and revised with the latest information from the U.S. Department of Labor, professional organizations, and other sources. In addition, the following new articles have been written specifically for this book: Horticulturists, Horticultural Inspectors, Nursery Owners and Managers, and Writers, Horticulture.

The following paragraphs detail the sections and features that appear in the book.

The **Quick Facts** section provides a brief summary of the career including recommended school subjects, personal skills, work environment, minimum educational requirements, salary ranges, certification or licensing requirements, and employment outlook. This section also provides acronyms and identification numbers for the following government classification indexes: the *Dictionary of*

Occupational Titles (DOT), the *Guide for Occupational Exploration* (GOE), the National Occupational Classification (NOC) Index, and the Occupational Information Network (O*NET)-Standard Occupational Classification System (SOC) index. The DOT, GOE, and O*NET-SOC indexes have been created by the U.S. government; the NOC index is Canada's career classification system. Readers can use the identification numbers listed in the Quick Facts section to access further information about a career. Print editions of the DOT (*Dictionary of Occupational Titles*. Indianapolis, Ind.: JIST Works, 1991) and GOE (*Guide for Occupational Exploration*. Indianapolis, Ind.: JIST Works, 2001) are available at libraries. Electronic versions of the NOC (http://www23.hrdc-drhc.gc.ca) and O*NET-SOC (http://online.onetcenter.org) are available on the Internet. When no DOT, GOE, NOC, or O*NET-SOC numbers are present, this means that the U.S. Department of Labor or Human Resources Development Canada have not created a numerical designation for this career. In this instance, you will see the acronym "N/A," or not available.

The **Overview** section is a brief introductory description of the duties and responsibilities involved in this career. Oftentimes, a career may have a variety of job titles. When this is the case, alternative career titles are presented. Employment statistics are also provided, when available. The **History** section describes the history of the particular job as it relates to the overall development of its industry or field. **The Job** describes the primary and secondary duties of the job. **Requirements** discusses high school and postsecondary education and training requirements, any certification or licensing that is necessary, and other personal requirements for success in the job. **Exploring** offers suggestions on how to gain experience in or knowledge of the particular job before making a firm educational and financial commitment. The focus is on what can be done while still in high school (or in the early years of college) to gain a better understanding of the job. The **Employers** section gives an overview of typical places of employment for the job. **Starting Out** discusses the best ways to land that first job, be it through the college career services office, newspaper ads, Internet employment sites, or personal contact. The **Advancement** section describes what kind of career path to expect from the job and how to get there. **Earnings** lists salary ranges and describes the typical fringe benefits. The **Work Environment** section describes the typical surroundings and conditions of employment—whether indoors or outdoors, noisy or quiet, social or independent. Also discussed are typical hours worked, any seasonal fluctuations, and the stresses and strains of the job. The

Outlook section summarizes the job in terms of the general economy and industry projections. For the most part, Outlook information is obtained from the U.S. Bureau of Labor Statistics and is supplemented by information gathered from professional associations. Job growth terms follow those used in the *Occupational Outlook Handbook*. Growth described as "much faster than the average" means an increase of 27 percent or more. Growth described as "faster than the average" means an increase of 18 to 26 percent. Growth described as "about as fast as the average" means an increase of 9 to 17 percent. Growth described as "more slowly than the average" means an increase of 0 to 8 percent. "Decline" means a decrease by any amount. Each article ends with **For More Information,** which lists organizations that provide information on training, education, internships, scholarships, and job placement.

Careers in Focus: Landscaping and Horticulture also includes photographs, informative sidebars, and interviews with professionals in the field.

Agricultural Scientists

OVERVIEW

Agricultural scientists study all aspects of living organisms and the relationships of plants and animals to their environment. They conduct basic research in laboratories or in the field. They apply the results to such tasks as increasing crop yields and improving the environment. Some agricultural scientists plan and administer programs for testing foods, drugs, and other products. Others direct activities at public exhibits at such places as zoos and botanical gardens. *Agricultural engineers* apply engineering principles to the food and agriculture industries. They design or develop agricultural equipment and machines, supervise production, and conduct tests on new designs and machine parts. Some agricultural scientists are professors at colleges and universities or work as consultants to business firms or the government. Others work in technical sales and service jobs for manufacturers of agricultural products. There are approximately 30,000 agricultural and food scientists in the United States; about 25 percent work for the federal, state, or local governments. Several thousand more are employed as university professors.

HISTORY

In 1840, Justius von Liebig of Germany published *Organic Chemistry in Its Applications to Agriculture and Physiology* and launched the systematic development of the agricultural sciences. A formal system of agricultural education soon followed in both Europe and the United States. Prior to the publication of this

QUICK FACTS

School Subjects
Agriculture
Biology
Chemistry

Personal Skills
Communication/ideas
Technical/scientific

Work Environment
Indoors and outdoors
Primarily multiple
 locations

Minimum Education Level
Bachelor's degree

Salary Range
$33,650 to $56,080 to
 $93,460+

Certification or Licensing
Voluntary (certification)
Required for certain posi-
 tions (licensing)

Outlook
About as fast as the average

DOT
040, 041

GOE
02.03.02, 02.07.01

NOC
2121

O*NET-SOC
17-2021.00, 19-1012.00,
 19-1013.00

work, agricultural developments relied on the collective experience of farmers handed down over generations. Agricultural science has techniques in common with many other disciplines including biology, botany, genetics, nutrition, breeding, and engineering. Discoveries and improvements in these fields contributed to advances in agriculture. Some milestones include the discovery of the practice of crop rotation and the application of manure as fertilizer, which greatly increased farm yields in the 1700s. Farm mechanization was greatly advanced by the invention of the mechanical reaper in 1831 and the gasoline tractor in 1892. Chemical fertilizers were first used in the 19th century; pesticides and herbicides soon followed. In 1900, the research of an Austrian monk, Gregor Johann Mendel, was rediscovered. His theories of plant characteristics, based on studies using generations of garden peas, formed the foundation for the science of genetics.

In the 20th century, scientists and engineers were at the forefront of farm, crop, and food processing improvements. Conservationist Gifford Pinchot developed some of the first methods to prevent soil erosion in 1910, and Clarence Birdseye perfected a method of freezing food in the 1920s. Birdseye's discoveries allowed for new crops of produce previously too perishable for the marketplace. Engineers in the 1930s developed more powerful farm machinery and scientists developed hybrid corn. By the 1960s, high-powered machinery and better quality feed and pesticides were in common use. Today, advances in genetic engineering and biotechnology are leading to more efficient, economical methods of farming and new markets for crops.

Agricultural scientists have also played an important role in the development of ethanol, a clean-burning fuel that is created from renewable resources such as corn. Some environmentalists are encouraging the use of ethanol as a means to reduce U.S. dependence on oil from foreign countries.

THE JOB

The nature of the work of the agricultural scientist can be broken down into several areas of specialization. Within each specialization there are various careers.

The following are careers that fall under the areas of plant and soil science.

Agronomists investigate large-scale food-crop problems, conduct experiments, and develop new methods of growing crops to ensure more efficient production, higher yields, and improved quality. They use genetic engineering to develop crops that are resistant to pests, drought, and plant diseases.

Agronomists also engage in soil science. They analyze soils to find ways to increase production and reduce soil erosion. They study the responses of various soil types to fertilizers, tillage practices, and crop rotation. Since soil science is related to environmental science, agronomists may also use their expertise to consult with farmers and agricultural companies on environmental quality and effective land use.

Botanists are concerned with plants and their environment, structure, heredity, and economic value in such fields as agronomy, horticulture, and medicine.

Horticulturists study fruit and nut orchards as well as garden plants such as vegetables and flowers. They conduct experiments to develop new and improved varieties and to increase crop quality and yields. They also work to improve plant culture methods for the landscaping and beautification of communities, parks, and homes.

Plant breeders apply genetics and biotechnology to improve plants' yield, quality, and resistance to harsh weather, disease, and insects. They might work on developing strains of wild or cultivated plants that will have a larger yield and increase profits.

Plant pathologists research plant diseases and the decay of plant products to identify symptoms, determine causes, and develop control measures. They attempt to predict outbreaks by studying how different soils, climates, and geography affect the spread and intensity of plant disease.

Food science is a specialty that focuses on meeting consumer demand for food products in ways that are healthy, safe, and convenient.

Food scientists use their backgrounds in chemistry, microbiology, and other sciences to develop new or better ways of preserving, packaging, processing, storing, and delivering foods. *Food technologists* work in product development to discover new food sources and analyze food content to determine levels of vitamins, fat, sugar, and protein. Food technologists also work to enforce government regulations, inspecting food processing areas and ensuring that sanitation, safety, quality, and waste management standards are met.

Another field related to agricultural science is agricultural engineering.

Agricultural engineers apply engineering principles to work in the food and agriculture industries. They design or develop agricultural equipment and machines, supervise production, and conduct tests on new designs and machine parts. They develop plans and specifications for agricultural buildings and for drainage and irrigation systems. They work on flood control, soil erosion, and land reclamation

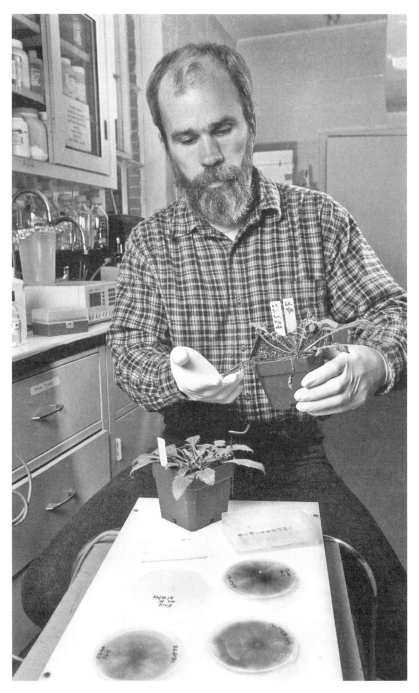

A plant pathologist conducts an experiment. *(Peggy Greb, Agricultural Research Service, U.S. Department of Agriculture)*

projects. They design food processing systems and equipment to convert farm products to consumer foods. Agricultural engineers contribute to making farming easier and more profitable through the introduction of new farm machinery and through advancements in soil and water conservation. Agricultural engineers in industry engage in research or in the design, testing, or sales of equipment.

Much of the research conducted by agricultural scientists is done in laboratories and requires a familiarity with research techniques and the use of laboratory equipment and computers. Some research, however, is carried out wherever necessary. A botanist may have occasion to examine the plants that grow in the volcanic valleys of Alaska, or an animal breeder may study the behavior of animals on the plains of Africa.

REQUIREMENTS

High School

Follow your high school's college preparatory program, which will include courses in English, foreign language, mathematics, and government. Also take biology, chemistry, physics, and any other science courses available. You must also become familiar with basic computer skills, including programming. It may be possible for you to perform laboratory assistant duties for your science teachers. Visiting research laboratories and attending lectures by agricultural scientists can also be helpful.

Postsecondary Training

Educational requirements for agricultural scientists are very high. A doctorate is usually mandatory for careers as college or university professors, independent researchers, or field managers. A bachelor's degree may be acceptable for some entry-level jobs, such as testing or inspecting technicians, or as technical sales or service representatives. Promotions, however, are very limited for these employees unless they earn advanced degrees.

To become an agricultural scientist, you should pursue a degree related to agricultural and biological science. As an undergraduate, you should have a firm foundation in biology, with courses in chemistry, physics, mathematics, and English. Most colleges and universities have agricultural science curriculums, although liberal arts colleges may emphasize the biological sciences. State universities usually offer agricultural science programs, too.

While pursuing an advanced degree, you'll participate in research projects and write a dissertation on your specialized area of study.

You'll also do fieldwork and laboratory research along with your classroom studies.

Certification or Licensing

The American Society of Agronomy offers several certifications, including the certified professional agronomist designation, to candidates based on their training and work. Contact the society for more information.

According to the American Society of Agricultural Engineers, agricultural engineers must hold an engineer's license.

Other Requirements

As a researcher, you should be self-motivated enough to work effectively alone, yet be able to function cooperatively as part of a team. You should have an inexhaustible curiosity about the nature of living things and their environments. You must be systematic in your work habits and in your approach to investigation and experimentation and must have the persistence to continue or start over when experiments are not immediately successful.

Work performed by agricultural scientists in offices and laboratories requires intense powers of concentration and the ability to communicate one's thoughts systematically. In addition to these skills, physical stamina is necessary for those scientists who do field research in remote areas of the world.

EXPLORING

If you live in an agricultural community, you may be able to find part-time or summer work on a farm or ranch. Joining a chapter of the National FFA Organization (formerly Future Farmers of America) or a 4-H program will introduce you to the concerns of farmers and researchers and may involve you directly in science projects. Contact your county's extension office to learn about regional projects. You may also find part-time work in veterinarian's offices, florist shops, landscape nurseries, orchards, farms, zoos, aquariums, botanical gardens, or museums. Volunteer work is often available in zoos and animal shelters.

EMPLOYERS

About 25 percent of all agricultural and food scientists work for federal, state, and local governments. They work within the U.S. Department of Agriculture and the Environmental Protection

Agency and for regional extension agencies and soil conservation departments. Scientists with doctorates may work on the faculty of colleges and universities. Researchers work for chemical and pharmaceutical companies, and with agribusiness and consulting firms. Agricultural scientists also work in the food processing industry.

STARTING OUT

Agricultural scientists often are recruited prior to graduation. College and university career services offices offer information about jobs, and students may arrange interviews with recruiters who visit the campus.

Direct application may be made to the personnel departments of colleges and universities, private industries, and nonprofit research foundations. People interested in positions with the federal government may contact the local offices of state employment services and the U.S. Office of Personnel Management (http://www.usajobs.opm.gov), which are located in various large cities throughout the country. Private employment agencies are another method that might be considered. Large companies sometimes conduct job fairs in major cities and will advertise them in the business sections of the local newspapers.

ADVANCEMENT

Advancement in this field depends on education, experience, and job performance. Agricultural scientists with advanced degrees generally start in teaching or research and advance to administrative and management positions, such as supervisor of a research program. The number of such jobs is limited, however, and often the route to advancement is through specialization. The narrower specialties are often the most valuable.

People who enter this field with only a bachelor's degree are much more restricted. After starting in testing and inspecting jobs or as technical sales and service representatives, they may progress to advanced technicians, particularly in medical research, or become high school biology teachers. In the latter case, they must have had courses in education and meet the state requirements for teaching credentials.

EARNINGS

According to the U.S. Department of Labor, the median annual salary of soil and plant scientists was approximately $56,080 in 2006. The lowest paid 10 percent (which generally included those just starting out in the field) earned less than $33,650, while the highest paid 10 percent made approximately $93,460 or more per year. Unless hired for just a short-term project, agricultural scientists most likely receive health and retirement benefits in addition to their annual salary.

WORK ENVIRONMENT

Agricultural scientists work regular hours, although researchers often choose to work longer when their experiments have reached critical points. Competition in the research field may be stiff, causing a certain amount of stress.

Agricultural scientists generally work in offices, laboratories, or classrooms where the environment is clean, healthy, and safe. Some agricultural scientists, such as botanists, periodically take field trips where living facilities may be primitive and strenuous physical activity may be required.

OUTLOOK

According to the U.S. Department of Labor, employment for agricultural scientists is expected to grow about as fast as the average for all occupations through 2014. The fields of biotechnology, genetics, and sustainable agriculture may hold the best opportunities for agricultural scientists. New developments, such as methods of processing corn for use in medicines and for fuel for motor vehicles, will alter the marketplace. Scientists will also be actively involved in improving both the environmental impact of farming and crop yields, as they focus on methods of decontaminating soil, protecting groundwater, crop rotation, and other efforts of conservation. Scientists will also have the challenge of promoting these new methods to farmers.

FOR MORE INFORMATION

To learn about careers and student competitions and scholarships, contact

American Society of Agricultural and Biological Engineers
2950 Niles Road
St. Joseph, MI 49085-8607
Tel: 269-429-0300
Email: hq@asabe.org
http://www.asabe.org

For information on careers and certification, contact
American Society of Agronomy
677 South Segoe Road
Madison, WI 53711-1086
Tel: 608-273-8080
http://www.agronomy.org

For more information on agricultural careers and student programs, contact
National FFA Organization
6060 FFA Drive
PO Box 68960
Indianapolis, IN 46268-0960
Tel: 317-802-6060
http://www.ffa.org

Visit the USDA Web site for more information on its agencies and programs as well as news releases.
United States Department of Agriculture (USDA)
1400 Independence Avenue, SW
Washington, DC 20250-0002
Tel: 202-720-2791
http://www.usda.gov

INTERVIEW

Doug Gasseling is a conservation agronomist for the Natural Resources Conservation Service (NRCS) of the U.S. Department of Agriculture. He has worked in the field for 35 years. Doug discussed his career with the editors of Careers in Focus: Landscaping and Horticulture.

Q. What are your main duties as a conservation agronomist?

A. As a conservation agronomist I am part of our state office for Wyoming. My current duties include working on keeping our *Electronic Field Office Technical Guide* up to date, reviewing conservation plans to certify our employees as certified planners, reviewing environmental impact statements (proposed projects) for how they will affect land uses the NRCS has an interest in, and training and assisting our field offices on planning.

Q. How did you train for this job? What was your college major?

A. I have a bachelor of science in agronomy. Training for this job was provided by the NRCS. As a new employee out of college, the employee is placed in an office that has a diverse workload and with an employee who has quite a bit of experience. This office is expected to train the new employee on how the NRCS does business. Many times this new employee will be in the office for one year, then move to another office with different land uses to be sure the individual is trained on all land uses (i.e., cropland, pastureland, hayland, and rangeland).

Q. What are the most important professional qualities for people in your career?

A. One important quality, although not necessary, is to have an agricultural or farm background. You also need to be a people-oriented person with good communication skills as most of your career is spent dealing with producers, conservation groups, and the general public.

Q. What advice would you give to young people who are interested in the field?

A. If you are interested in work with the NRCS, once employed, be patient and learn as much as you can from the personnel who are training you. Do not try to advance too fast; if this happens, it could hurt your career in that you get in a position before you are ready or have the knowledge to do the job. With the NRCS you may be working in a lot of other positions prior to being able to do what a true agronomist would do. This is part of learning and the advancement process.

Arborists

OVERVIEW

Arborists are professionals who practice arboriculture, which is the care of trees and shrubs, especially those found in urban areas. Arborists prune and fertilize trees and other woody plants as well as monitor them for insects and diseases. Arborists are often consulted for various tree-related issues. Approximately 55,000 arborists are employed in the United States.

HISTORY

Arboriculture developed as a branch of the plant science of horticulture. While related to the study of forestry, arborists view their specimens on an individual level; foresters manage trees as a group.

Trees are important to our environment. Besides releasing oxygen back to our atmosphere, trees enrich our soil with their fallen, decaying leaves, and their roots aid in the prevention of soil erosion. Trees provide shelter and a source of food for many different types of animals. People use trees as ornamentation. Trees are often planted to protect against the wind and glare of the sun, block offensive views, mark property lines, and provide privacy. Trees and shrubs often add considerably to a home's property value.

All trees need proper care and seasonal maintenance. The occupation of *tree surgeon,* as arborists were first known, came from the need for qualified individuals to care for trees and shrubs, as well as woody vines and ground-cover plants. Trees planted in busy city areas and in the suburbs face pollution, traffic, crowding, extreme temperatures, and other daily hazards. City trees often have a large percentage of their roots covered with concrete. Roots of larger trees sometimes interfere with plumbing pipes, sidewalks, and building foundations. Branches can interfere with buildings or power lines. Trees located along the sides of roads and highways must be maintained; branches are pruned, and fallen leaves and fruit are gathered. Proper intervention, if not prevention, of diseases is an important task of arborists.

THE JOB

Trees and shrubs need more than just sunlight and water. That's where arborists take over. Arborists perform many different tasks for trees and shrubs, some for the sake of maintenance and others for the tree's health and well-being.

Pruning. All trees need some amount of pruning to control their shape; sometimes limbs are trimmed if they interfere with power lines, if they cross property lines, or if they grow too close to houses and other buildings. Arborists may use tools such as pruning shears or hand and power saws to do the actual cutting. If the branches are especially large or cumbersome, arborists may rope them together before the sawing begins. After cutting, the branches can be safely lowered to the ground. Ladders, aerial lifts, and cranes may be used to reach extremely tall trees. Sometimes, arborists need to cable or brace tree limbs weakened by disease or old age or damaged by a storm.

Planting or transplanting. When cities or towns plan a new development, or wish to gentrify an existing one, they often consult with arborists to determine what types of trees to plant. Arborists can suggest trees that will thrive in a certain environment. Young plantings, or immature trees, are more cost effective and are often used, though sometimes, larger, more mature trees are transplanted to the desired location.

Diagnosis and treatment. A large part of keeping a tree healthy is the prevention of disease. There are a number of diseases that affect trees, among them anthracnose and Dutch elm disease. Insects pose a potential threat to trees, and have done considerable damage to certain species in the past, by boring into the trunk or spreading disease-causing organisms. Bacteria, fungi, viruses, and disease-causing organisms can also be fatal enemies of trees. Arborists are specially trained to identify the insect or the disease weakening the tree and apply the necessary remedy or medication. Common methods prescribed by arborists include chemical insecticides, or the use of natural insect predators to combat the problem. Arborists closely monitor insect migrations or any other situations that may be harmful to a species of tree.

When a tree is too old or badly diseased, arborists may choose to cut it down. Arborists will carefully cut the tree into pieces to prevent injury to people or damage to surrounding property.

Arborists must be in excellent physical shape and unafraid of heights. *(PhotoDisc)*

Prevention. Trees, especially young plantings, often need extra nourishment. Arborists are trained to apply fertilizers, both natural and chemical, in a safe and environmentally friendly manner. Arborists are also hired by golf courses and parks to install lightning protection systems for lone trees or mature, valuable trees.

REQUIREMENTS

High School

High school biology, earth science, and environmental science classes can provide you with a solid background to be a successful arborist. An interest in gardening, conservation, or the outdoors is also helpful.

Postsecondary Training

Take classes in botany, chemistry, horticulture, and plant pathology. Several colleges and universities offer programs in arboriculture and other related fields such as landscape design, nursery stock production, or grounds and turf maintenance. Entry-level positions such as assistants or climbers do not need a college degree for employment. Advanced education, however, is highly desired if you plan to make this field your career.

Certification or Licensing

The Tree Care Industry Association (TCIA) and the International Society of Arboriculture (ISA) both offer various home study courses and books on arboriculture. Most arborists are certified or licensed. Licensure ensures an arborist meets the state's regulations for working with pesticides and herbicides. Check with your local government—not all states require arborists to be licensed. Certification, given by the ISA after completion of required training and education, is considered by many as a measure of an arborist's skill and experience in the industry. Today's savvy consumers specifically look for certified arborists when it comes to caring for their trees and other precious landscaping plants. The ISA offers the following certification designations to arborists: board certified master arborist, certified arborist, certified arborist/utility specialist, certified arborist/municipal specialist, and certified tree worker/climber specialist.

EXPLORING

Interested in this field? Surfing the Internet can provide a wealth of information for you to browse. Log onto the Web sites of the TCIA or ISA for industry and career information. If you really want to test the waters, why not find summer work with an arborist? You'll earn extra spending money while at the same time learning about the industry firsthand. Check with the TCIA for a complete listing of certified arborists in your area.

EMPLOYERS

Approximately 55,000 arborists are employed in the United States. Landscaping companies and businesses that offer a host of expert tree services are common employers of arborists. Employment opportunities are also available with municipal governments, botanical gardens, and arboretums. For example, an arborist in the Chicago area may want to seek a position with the Chicago Botanic Garden or the Morton Arboretum; both places are known for their lush gardens and wooded trails.

STARTING OUT

So you've decided to become an arborist—what's the next step? Start by compiling a list of tree care firms in your area, then send your resume or fill out an application with the companies that interest you. You should also consider employment with the highway or park department of your city or county—they often hire crews to maintain their trees.

Tools of the Trade

Tree Climbing Equipment
- Ascenders/rope grabs
- Carabiners/clips
- Climbers
- Harnesses
- Rigging Gear
- Rope (multiple varieties)
- Saddles
- Spurs

Heavy Machinery
- Chippers
- Grinders
- Portable winches

Cutting Implements
- Axes
- Chainsaws
- Pole Saws
- Gas Pruners
- Hand Pruners
- Pole Pruners
- Hand Saws
- Knives
- Pneumatic Tools

Other
- Hard hats
- Protective clothing

Many colleges and universities offer job placement services, or they at least post employment opportunities in their office. Industry associations and trade magazines are often good sources of job openings.

Don't plan to climb to the top of an American elm your first day on the job. Expect to stay at ground level, at least for a few days. Trainees in this industry start as *helpers* or *ground workers,* who load and unload equipment from trucks, gather branches and other debris for disposal, handle ropes, and give assistance to climbers. They also operate the chipper—a machine that cuts large branches into small chips. After some time observing more experienced workers, trainees are allowed to climb smaller trees or the lower limbs of large trees. They are also taught the proper way to operate large machinery and climbing gear. Most companies provide on-the-job training that lasts from one to three months.

ADVANCEMENT

Experienced arborists can advance to supervisory positions such as crew manager or department supervisor. Another option is to become a consultant in the field and work for tree care firms, city or town boards, large nurseries, or gardening groups.

Arborists with a strong entrepreneurial nature can choose to open their own business, but aspiring entrepreneurs must make sure that their business skills are up to par. Even the most talented and hardworking arborists won't stand a chance if they can't balance their accounts or market their services properly.

Advancement to other industries related to arboriculture is another possibility. Some arborists choose to work in landscape design, forestry, or other fields of horticulture.

EARNINGS

The U.S. Department of Labor lists the median yearly salary of tree trimmers and pruners as $28,250 in 2006. The bottom 10 percent earned $18,720 a year or less, and the top 10 percent earned $44,350 a year or more.

According to the ISA, entry-level positions, such as grounds workers or trainees, can earn between $7 to $10 an hour; supervisors, with three or more years of experience, earn from $20 to $30 an hour; private consultants with eight to 10 years of experience, or arborists in sales positions, can earn $50,000 to $60,000 or more annually. Salaries vary greatly depending on many factors, among them the size of the company, the region, and the experience of the arborist. Arborists servicing busy urban areas tend to earn more.

Full-time employees receive a benefits package including health insurance, life insurance, paid vacation and sick time, and paid holidays. Most tree companies supply necessary uniforms, tools, equipment, and training.

WORK ENVIRONMENT

Much of an arborist's work is physically demanding, and most of it is done outdoors. Arborists work throughout the year, though their busiest time is in the spring and summer. Tasks done at this time include fertilizing, pruning, and prevention spraying. During the winter months, arborists can expect to care for trees injured or damaged by excess snow, ice storms, or floods.

Equipment such as sharp saws, grinders, chippers, bulldozers, tractors, and other large machinery can be potentially dangerous for arborists. There is also the risk of falling from the top of a tall tree, many of which reach heights of 50 feet or more. Arborists rely on cleated shoes, security belts, and safety hoists to make their job easier as well as safer.

OUTLOOK

The future of arboriculture has never looked so promising. The U.S Department of Labor predicts faster than average growth for this field through 2014. The public's increasing interest in the planning and the preservation of the environment has increased demand for qualified arborists. Many homeowners are willing to pay top dollar for professionally designed and maintained landscaping. Increased resistance to pesticides and new species of insects pose constant threats to all trees. While travel abroad is easier and, in a sense, has made our world smaller, it has also placed our environment at risk. For example, Asian long-horn beetles were unknowingly transported to the United States via packing material. By the time the insects were discovered, the beetles had irreversibly damaged hundreds of mature trees throughout New York, Chicago, and surrounding areas. Arborists, especially those trained to diagnose and treat such cases, will be in demand to work in urban areas.

FOR MORE INFORMATION

For industry and career information, or to receive a copy of Arborist News *or* Careers in Arboriculture, *contact*
International Society of Arboriculture
PO Box 3129
Champaign, IL 61826-3129
Tel: 888-472-8733
Email: isa@isa-arbor.com
http://www.isa-arbor.com

For industry information and membership requirements, contact
Society of Municipal Arborists
PO Box 641
Watkinsville, GA 30677-0015
Tel: 706-769-7412
Email: urbanforestry@prodigy.net
http://www.urban-forestry.com

For industry and career information, a listing of practicing arborists, or educational programs at the university level, or home study, contact
Tree Care Industry Association
Three Perimeter Road, Unit 1
Manchester, NH 03103-3341
Tel: 800-733-2622
http://www.treecareindustry.org

INTERVIEW

Tchukki Andersen is the staff arborist for the Tree Care Industry Association. She discussed her career with the editors of Careers in Focus: Landscaping and Horticulture.

Q. What is the one thing that many people might not know about the work of arborists?

A. It is very diverse. There are many different callings for arborists, from actual tree work to urban forestry and planning to consulting to biomass products. Arborists are no longer expected to simply remove trees. They need to know tree growth and structure, tree laws, rigging and engineering, cultivar selection and planting, and have good communication skills in order to make potentially substantial wages and to stay safe while doing so.

Q. What made you want to become an arborist?

A. After college I started out mowing lawns to give me a little bit of money so I could race outrigger canoes. Mowing lawns quickly turned into pruning trees and shrubs, which I decided I liked much more. I worked as a practicing arborist (actually pruning and caring for trees) for 16 years. I just recently hung up my full-time pruning saws to become the staff arborist for the Tree Care Industry Association (TCIA).

Q. What are your main duties as a staff arborist?

A. I answer phone calls and e-mails from people all over the country who have questions regarding tree care. I talk with homeowners, tree professionals, and arboricultural researchers regularly about their tree questions. I also prepare the content for the *TreeWorker,* a newsletter for tree workers who are members of the TCIA and/or arborists in general who subscribe to the publication. I give presentations to interested groups of people about topical issues in arboriculture, and offer ideas to the TCIA about how its member tree companies can better serve those interested groups.

Q. How did you train for this job? What was your college major or did you train in another way?

A. Train to become an arborist? I kind of went at it backwards. I graduated from Eastern Washington University with a bachelor of arts in music theory, which had nothing to do with trees. Then I started mowing lawns and pruning smaller trees. I taught myself a lot of the profession. About 10 years into it, I decided I needed more education as an arborist because of all the industry changes, so I went back to school for my associate's degree in forest resource technologies.

So I have a bachelor of arts in music theory, which, believe it or not, has opened a lot of doors for me, and I have an associate of science degree in forest resource technologies.

Q. What are the most important professional qualities for arborists?

A. Good ethics. Someone who takes the steps to educate themselves, and can present that image to a customer. Someone who is honest, doesn't overcharge or steal, or show up late.

Ongoing education is very important because industry research is constantly presenting new information to the people interested enough to learn it and get ahead in this business.

Q. What advice would you give to young people who are interested in the field?

A. Be open to anything that comes along as far as work goes. Become well rounded in your experience and education, and eventually it will pay off with a job that you love at a decent rate of pay.

Q. Can you tell us about the work of the Tree Care Industry Association?

A. The TCIA accredits tree care companies, develops safety and education programs, establishes standards of tree care practice, and provides management information for arboriculture firms around the world. We provide continuing education, training, conferences, and publications to promote the safe and appropriate practice of tree care. The TCIA produces *Tree Care Industry* magazine, the most circulated and read publication in the industry, and TCI EXPO, the world's largest tree care trade show.

Beekeepers

OVERVIEW

Beekeepers, also known as *apiarists*, care for and raise honeybees for commercial and agricultural purposes, such as honey production and crop pollination. Their duties might include assembling beehives and other equipment, buying and selling bees, establishing settlements close to pollination-dependent crops, transporting wild beehives to a central location, raising queen bees, and harvesting and selling honey. Beekeepers may work on farms or small plots of land to raise bees to assist in the production of grain and other agricultural crops. It is said that one-third of food production in the United States depends on bees. Beekeeping may be a full-time job, a "sideline" job, or a hobby. Beekeepers usually work alone or as a member of a small team.

HISTORY

Early rock paintings in Spain and Africa depict people gathering honey from trees or rock crevices while bees flew around them. Ancient Egyptian relics show the beekeeper taking honey from a hive while a helper drives the bees away with smoke. There is evidence that the Mayans kept a stingless, honey-storing bee. Relics from Belize and Mexico, including stone disks thought to have been the end stoppers on wooden, log-shaped hives, represent the oldest artifacts related to beekeeping in the New World.

Early honey gatherers probably accidentally discovered that smoke calms bees when they used fire to drive off other animals. Beekeeping may have originally developed following the observation that swarms of bees will settle in any container with a dark, protected

QUICK FACTS

School Subjects
Agriculture
Biology
Earth science

Personal Skills
Mechanical/manipulative
Technical/scientific

Work Environment
Primarily outdoors
One location with some
 travel

Minimum Education Level
Apprenticeship

Salary Range
$0 to $10,000 to $20,000

Certification or Licensing
Required by certain states

Outlook
Decline

DOT
413

GOE
03.01.01

NOC
8251

O*NET-SOC
11-9012.00

interior space. Pottery and natural containers, such as holes in trees or logs, provide shelter and protection for hive establishment. In some forested areas of Europe, hive clusters made from logs can still be found. Horizontal pottery hives are used along the Mediterranean, and straw hives, known as "skeps," are still used in Belgium and France.

The honeybee, which is not native to North America, was shipped to the colonies from England in the first half of the 17th century. For many years, straw skeps were used for hives, followed by log "gums." With these crude hives, it was difficult to know when the bees had problems with disease or starvation or if they were queenless; the beekeeper could not inspect the combs to determine what was wrong. By the same token, it was difficult to extract honey from these hives without damaging or destroying the bee colony. Typically, beekeepers had to kill their swarms each fall by burning sulphur at the entrance of the hive; then the honey and beeswax could be removed.

In the 17th and 18th centuries, beekeepers began to build movable-comb hives, which enabled them to inspect combs without damaging them. In 1789, Francis Huber invented the first movable-frame hive. The combs in this hive could be easily inspected like the pages of a book. In 1852, Lorenzo Langstroth, a minister from Pennsylvania, patented a hive with movable frames that hung from the top of the hive, leaving a 3/8-inch space between the frames and the hive body (the exact spacing at which bees will build comb they can move around, referred to today as "beespace"). By the turn of the 20th century, most beekeepers were using Langstroth's system. Langstroth is known as "the father of modern beekeeping."

Modern beekeeping methods evolved very rapidly following the invention of Langstroth's system. Wax-comb foundation, which made possible the consistent production of high-quality combs of worker cells, was invented in 1857. The centrifugal honey extractor was invented in 1865, enabling large-scale production of honey, and later in the century the radial extractor (where both sides of the frame are extracted at the same time) was invented. In 1889, G. M. Doolittle of New York developed the system for rearing queen bees that is still used today by all commercial queen-rearers. Bee smokers and veils evolved and improved. Also around this time, leaders in American beekeeping learned of the merits of the Italian honeybee, and they began to import these bees into the states. Today, the American version of the Italian honeybee is still widely used throughout the country.

A beekeeper (left) and geneticist inspect a colony of Russian honey bees. *(Scott Bauer, Agricultural Research Service, U.S. Department of Agriculture)*

Today the most significant advances in beekeeping are related to the areas of bee management and the extracting process. In general, the dimensions of hives and frames have become more standardized, drugs are available for disease control, artificial insemination of queen bees is being used commercially, and colony rental is being used increasingly for crop pollination.

THE JOB

In the spring, beekeepers set up new hives and repair old ones. A beginning beekeeper will have to purchase bees from a dealer. The beekeeper will set up the hive near an orchard or field where nectar will be available for the bees.

A beekeeper's primary task is the care and feeding of the bees. The hives must be inspected regularly for mite infestations and diseases. The bees must also occasionally be fed, especially during the winter months when forage is unavailable.

Beekeepers ensure that the bees and their surroundings are healthy and clean. They watch out for robber bees, who will try to rob food from other hives when they are unable to find enough nectar to make honey. Beekeepers make it easier for the bees to defend the hive by limiting the size of the entrance. Beekeepers must also watch for "swarming," a situation in which about half of the bees from a colony look for a new place to live because the hive has become too crowded or is no longer adequately ventilated. To prevent swarming, the entrance to the hive can be enlarged to improve air circulation, especially during the summer. The beekeeper might also clip the queen's wings to prevent her from leaving with the swarm or move half the bees to a new hive with another queen.

The queen bee also requires special attention. In a properly functioning hive the queen will be almost constantly laying eggs. If she becomes sick or old, the beekeeper will need to replace her.

Beekeepers must wear special equipment when working with bees. A veil and plastic helmet protect the beekeeper's head and neck from the stings of angry bees. Some beekeepers also wear thick clothing and gloves for protection, although many professionals feel that the thick clothes are too bulky and hot. Their choice is to risk the occasional sting to gain the benefit of wearing lighter clothing.

A beekeeper uses smoke to keep the bees from swarming in anger. An angry bee gives off a scent that alarms the rest of the hive. Smoke, produced in a special smoker device, masks the alarm scent, preventing the formation of an attack swarm.

Beekeepers must purchase or construct special enclosures to contain the beehives. The most popular model in the United States is the Langstroth hive, a rectangular wood and metal construction that sits upon a stand to keep it dry.

Harvesting honey is an important part of the beekeeper's job. When the honey is ready for harvesting, beekeepers seal the honeycomb with beeswax. They remove the frames of honeycombs and take them to the extractor, where the honey is spun out of the honeycomb. It is filtered and drained into a tank. The honey is stored in five-gallon buckets or in 55-gallon drums. This is a part of beekeeping where physical strength is important.

Beekeepers also spend time keeping data on their colonies. Their records track information regarding the queens, any extra food that may have been required, honey yields and dates, and so forth.

REQUIREMENTS

High School

If you're interested in beekeeping, you should take high school classes in business and mathematics to prepare you for the records-keeping aspect of this work. Science classes, such as natural sciences, biology, and earth science, will give you an understanding of the environment as well as processes such as pollination. If your high school offers agriculture classes, be sure to take those for added understanding of crop and animal production. Wood shop classes will also be useful if you intend to build your own hives.

Postsecondary Training
Many people learn to do this work by getting informal on-the-job training when working with an experienced beekeeper. Community or junior colleges that offer agriculture classes may also provide another avenue for learning about honey production and bee care. Finally, some states may offer apprenticeship programs in beekeeping. To find out what agency to contact in your state regarding apprenticeships, visit the Employment and Training Administration's Web site at http://www.doleta.gov.

Certification or Licensing
Beekeeping licenses are issued at the state level, and requirements vary from state to state. Some states do not require a license at all, although almost every state requires that the commercial beekeeper register every hive.

Other Requirements
While a love of nature and the ability and desire to work alone were once among the most important characteristics for a beekeeper, many beekeepers today feel that a shrewd business sense and marketing savvy are what's most necessary to survive. Most commercial beekeepers seem to agree that the key to success as a beekeeper lies less in working with the bees than in working in the commercial business marketplace. Therefore, a good understanding of economics and basic business accounting is essential to the practice of beekeeping.

Top Honey-Producing States, 2006

1. North Dakota	6. Minnesota
2. California	7. Wisconsin
3. Florida	8. Texas
4. South Dakota	9. Georgia
5. Montana	10. Idaho

Source: National Agricultural Statistics Service, U.S. Department of Agriculture

Nevertheless, beekeepers still need physical strength, endurance, and a love of the outdoors to be successful. Of course, a beekeeper will also be working with large groups of insects, so this is not a job for people with aversions to insects or allergies to bee venom.

EXPLORING

If you are interested in beekeeping, you should contact a local bee-keeping association for advice and guidance. You should find an experienced, successful beekeeper who is willing to share his or her knowledge. A part-time job with a beekeeper would be an ideal introduction to the trade, but the opportunity simply to observe a beekeeper and ask questions is also invaluable. Read as much as you can about beekeeping. Start by checking out your local library for books on the subject; look for books written specifically for your part of the country. You should also subscribe to a beekeeping maga-zine, such as *BeeCulture* (http://www.beeculture.com) or *American Bee Journal* (http://www.dadant.com/journal). Join a local chapter of 4-H or the National FFA (formerly Future Farmers of America). While you may not gain direct experience with beekeeping, you will be able to work on agricultural or other projects and gain manage-ment experience.

EMPLOYERS

Beekeeping is a small and specialized profession. Some in the field estimate that there are under 2,000 professional beekeepers in the United States. The vast majority of beekeepers today do not depend on beekeeping for their income; they're known in the trade as "side-liners" or hobbyists. Most beekeepers run their own independent business rather than work for a large commercial establishment.

STARTING OUT

Since most beekeepers work independently, the most likely route of entry is to learn the basics and invest in some starting equipment. You can contact your local beekeeping association for advice. Keep in mind that if you hope to raise bees for commercial profit, you will need a substantial amount of capital to get started, and you're likely to face several years without profits while you work to increase honey production. If you live in an area where bees are raised, you should contact local beekeepers who may hire you for part-time or seasonal work.

ADVANCEMENT

Advancement in this field most often comes as beekeepers increase the number of hives they own and increase their commercial sales. It isn't likely that new beekeepers will be able to support themselves by beekeeping alone; most likely it will be a hobby or a sideline to supplement their living.

EARNINGS

Earnings for beekeepers vary greatly, even from year to year, as honey prices fluctuate and production from hives changes. Other variables that affect earnings include the number of hives a beekeeper has, the type of honey produced, and the season's weather conditions. Some beekeepers end up with no profits. Commercial beekeepers may only make in the $10,000 to $20,000 range. The National Agricultural Statistics Service reports the average price paid for the honey crop was approximately $1.04 per pound in 2006, and colonies averaged a production of 64.7 pounds. This means that a beekeeper could potentially earn about $67 from every colony owned. Remember, however, expenses and taxes have not been subtracted from this amount. To make a profit, a beekeeper typically needs to have thousands of colonies producing well. Medium and small sized operations usually have a difficult time turning any profit.

Some beekeepers are able to earn income through raising hives to rent to crop growers. Rental fees vary, but it's not unusual for a beekeeper to get $40 to $50 per hive for a two- to three-week period. Some small-scale beekeepers are able to market and sell specialty items (for example, beeswax-based products) that can be profitable, but again, this is usually a hobby or sideline, not an exclusive source of income.

WORK ENVIRONMENT

Beekeepers work primarily outdoors. The "in-season" hours (mostly in the spring and summer) can be very long, and the work can be physically challenging. Those who enjoy nature might well be suited for beekeeping, but there are indoor components to the work as well, such as tending to business records, processing honey, and caring for equipment. This is a field that requires discipline and the ability to work without supervision. A beekeeper must spend many hours working alone in tasks that can be grueling. Many beekeepers work part time at the trade while performing other agricultural duties.

Those with a sensitivity to bee stings should certainly avoid this industry, as—despite protective gear—stings are an inevitable part of the job.

OUTLOOK

Since the 1980s, 90 percent of the nation's wild honeybees have been wiped out by tracheal and varroa mites. Additionally, Colony Collapse Disorder, which is characterized by sudden colony death, has decimated honeybee colonies across the United States in recent years. As a result of these developments, many beekeepers find that their bee colonies dwindle by over half each year, while costs are up as much as 100 percent. With less than 2,000 commercial beekeepers currently in operation in the United States and one-third of our food supply dependent on honeybees for pollination, it might seem logical to assume that there will be increasing demand for their services in the future. However, since the North American Free Trade Agreement was passed, the need for orchard pollination services has shifted from the United States to Mexico. In addition, it is increasingly difficult for domestic producers to compete with the prices of imported honey. Foreign honey producers have fewer environmental regulations to abide by, lower wage rates to pay, and fewer worker benefits to provide. Thus, they are able to charge less for their product. Due to all of these factors, beekeepers in the United States are seeing demand for their services in decline. However, many continue to keep bees as a hobby or sideline business.

FOR MORE INFORMATION

The American Beekeeping Federation acts on behalf of the beekeeping industry on issues affecting the interests and the economic viability of the various sectors of the industry. The organization sponsors an essay contest in conjunction with 4-H and also has a Honey Queen and Honey Princess Program. For more information, contact

American Beekeeping Federation
PO Box 1337
Jesup, GA 31598-1038
Tel: 912-427-4233
Email: info@abfnet.org
http://www.abfnet.org

For information on the programs offered by these organizations and how to join, contact

National 4-H Headquarters
U.S. Department of Agriculture
Cooperative State Research, Education, and Extension Service
1400 Independence Avenue, SW, Stop 2225
Washington, DC 20250-2225
Tel: 202-720-2908
Email: 4hhq@csrees.usda.gov
http://www.national4-hheadquarters.gov
http://www.4husa.org

National FFA Organization
6060 FFA Drive
PO Box 68960
Indianapolis, IN 46268-0960
Tel: 317-802-6060
http://www.ffa.org

The National Honey Board serves the honey industry by increasing demand for honey and honey products. Check out its Web site for information on the industry.

National Honey Board
11409 Business Park Circle, Suite 210
Firestone, CO 80504-9203
Tel: 303-776-2337
http://www.honey.com/honeyindustry

The Backyard Beekeepers Association is a national club that provides its membership with interesting and practical information about the "how-to's" of beekeeping. The club also provides the general public with educational programs about honeybees and the benefits of beekeeping in the community. Visit its Web site to locate a club near you.

Backyard Beekeepers Association
http://www.backyardbeekeepers.com

Botanists

OVERVIEW

Botanists study all different aspects of plant life, from cellular structure to reproduction, to how plants are distributed, to how rainfall or other conditions affect them, and more. Botany is an integral part of modern science and industry, with diverse applications in agriculture, agronomy (soil and crop science), conservation, manufacturing, forestry, horticulture, and other areas. Botanists work for the government, in research and teaching institutions, and for private industry. The primary task of botanists is research and applied research. Nonresearch jobs in testing and inspection, or as lab technicians/technical assistants, also are available. Botany is an extremely diverse field with many specialties.

HISTORY

Plant science is hundreds of years old. The invention of microscopes in the 1600s was very important to the development of modern botany. Microscopes allowed minute study of plant anatomy and cells and led to considerable research in the field. It was in the 1600s that people started using words like *botanographist* or *botanologist*, for one who describes plants.

In the 1700s, Carolus Linnaeus, a Swedish botanist and *taxonomist* (one who identifies, names, and classifies plants) was an important figure. He came up with the two-name (genus and species) system for describing plants that is still used today. In all, Linnaeus wrote more than 180 works on plants, plant diseases, and related subjects.

In Austria during the 19th century monk Gregor Johann Mendel did the first experiments in hybridization. He experimented on garden peas and other plants to figure out why organisms inherit the traits they do. His work is the basis for 20th and 21st century work in plant and animal genetics. As interest in botany grew, botanical gardens became popular in Europe and North America.

Botany is a major branch of biology; the other is zoology. Today, studies in botany reach into many areas of biology, including genetics, biophysics, and other specialized studies. It has taken on particular urgency as a potential source of help for creating new drugs to fight disease, meeting food needs of developing countries, and battling environmental problems.

THE JOB

Research and applied research are the primary tasks of botanists. Literally every aspect of plant life is studied: cell structure, anatomy, heredity, reproduction, and growth; how plants are distributed on the earth; how rainfall, climate, soil, elevation, and other conditions affect plants; and how humans can put plants to better use. In most cases, botanists work at a specific problem or set of problems in their research. For example, they may develop new varieties of crops that will better resist disease. Some botanists focus on a specific type of plant species, such as fungi (mycology), or plants that are native to a specific area, such as a forest or prairie. A botanist working in private industry, for example, for a food or drug company, may focus on the development of new products, testing and inspection, regulatory compliance, or other areas.

Research takes place in laboratories, experiment stations (research sites found at many universities), botanical gardens, and other facilities. Powerful microscopes and special mounting, staining, and preserving techniques may be used in this sort of research.

Some botanists, particularly those working in conservation or ecological areas, also go out into the field. They inventory species, help re-create lost or damaged ecosystems, or direct pollution cleanup efforts.

Nonresearch jobs in testing and inspection or as lab technicians/technical assistants for universities, museums, government agencies, parks, manufacturing companies, botanical gardens, and other facilities also are available.

Botany is an extremely diverse field with many specialties. *Ethnobotanists* study the use of plant life by a particular culture, people, or ethnic group to find medicinal uses of certain plants. Study of traditional Native American medicinal uses of plants is an example.

Forest ecologists focus on forest species and their habitats, such as forest wetlands. Related studies include forest genetics and forest economics. Jobs in forestry include work in managing, maintaining, and improving forest species and environments.

Mycologists study fungi and apply their findings in agriculture, medicine, and industry for development of drugs, medicines, molds, and yeasts. They may specialize in research and development in a field such as antibiotics.

Toxicologists study the effect of toxic substances on organisms, including plants. Results of their work may be used in regulatory action, product labeling, and other areas.

Other botanical specialists include *morphologists,* who study macroscopic plant forms and life cycles; *palyologists,* who study pollen and spores; *pteridologists,* who study ferns and other related plants; *bryologists,* who study mosses and similar plants; and *lichenologists,* who study lichens, which are dual organisms made of both alga and fungus.

REQUIREMENTS

High School

To prepare for a career in botany, high school students can explore their interests by taking biology, doing science projects involving plants, and working during summers or school holidays for a nursery, park, or similar operation. College prep courses in chemistry, physics, biology, mathematics, English, and foreign language are a good idea because educational requirements for professional botanists are high. Nonresearch jobs (test and inspection professionals, lab technicians, technical assistants) require at least a bachelor's degree in a biological science or botany; research and teaching positions usually require at least a master's degree or even a doctorate.

Postsecondary Training

At the undergraduate level, there are numerous programs for degrees in botany or biology (which includes studies in both botany and zoology). The master's level and above usually involves a specialized degree. One newer degree is conservation biology, which focuses on the conservation of specific plant and animal communities. The University of Wisconsin–Madison (http://www.nelson.wisc.edu/grad/cbsd) has one of the biggest programs in the United States. Another key school is Yale University's School of Forestry and Environmental

Studies (http://environment.yale.edu), which offers degrees in areas such as natural resource management.

Other Requirements
Botanists chose their profession because of their love for plants, gardening, and nature. They need patience, an exploring spirit, the ability to work well alone or with other people, good writing and other communication skills, and tenacity.

EXPLORING

The Botanical Society of America (BSA) suggests that high school students take part in science fairs and clubs and get summer jobs with parks, nurseries, farms, experiment stations, labs, camps, florists, or landscape architects. Hobbies like camping, photography, and computers are useful, too, says the BSA. Tour a botanical garden in your area and talk to staff. You can also get information by contacting national associations. For example, visit the Botanical Society of America's Web site (http://www.botany.org) to read a brochure on careers in botany.

EMPLOYERS

Botanists find employment in the government, in research and teaching institutions, and in private industry. Local, state, and federal agencies, including the Department of Agriculture, Environmental Protection Agency, Public Health Service, Biological Resources Discipline, and the National Aeronautics and Space Administration employ botanists. Countless colleges and universities have botany departments and conduct botanical research. In private industry, botanists work for agribusiness, biotechnology, biological supply, chemical, environmental, food, lumber and paper, pharmaceutical, and petrochemical companies. Botanists also work for greenhouses, arboretums, herbariums, seed and nursery companies, and fruit growers.

STARTING OUT

With a bachelor's degree, a botanist's first job may be as a technical assistant or technician for a lab. Those with a master's degree might get work on a university research project. Someone with a doctorate might get into research and development with a drug, pharmaceutical, or other manufacturer.

For some positions, contract work might be necessary before the botanist gains a full-time position. Contract work is work done on a per-project, or freelance, basis: You sign on for that one project, and then you move on. Conservation groups like The Nature Conservancy (TNC) hire hundreds of contract workers, including ecologists and botanists, each year to do certain work. Contract workers are especially in demand in the summer when there's a lot of biology inventory work to be done.

Opportunities for internships are available with local chapters of TNC. It's also possible to volunteer. Contact the Student Conservation Association for volunteer opportunities. (Contact information can be found at the end of this article.) Land trusts are also good places to check for volunteer work.

ADVANCEMENT

Federal employees generally move up the ranks after gaining a certain number of hours of experience and obtaining advanced degrees. The Botanical Society of America, whose membership primarily comes from universities, notes that key steps for advancing in university positions include producing quality research, publishing a lot, and obtaining advanced degrees. Advancing in the private sector depends on the individual employer. Whatever the botanist can do to contribute to the bottom line, such as making breakthroughs in new product development, improving growing methods, and creating better test and inspection methods, will probably help the botanist advance in the company.

EARNINGS

According to the U.S. Department of Labor, the median annual salary of soil and plant scientists was approximately $56,080 in 2006. The lowest paid 10 percent (which generally included those just starting out in the field) earned less than $33,650, while the highest paid 10 percent made approximately $93,460 or more per year. Biological scientists, which include botanists, had annual incomes ranging from $40,820 to $129,510 in 2006. According to the National Association of Colleges and Employers, in 2005 graduates with a bachelor's degree in biological sciences received average starting salary offers of $31,258 a year; those with master's degrees received offers of $33,600, and those with Ph.D.'s received offers of $42,244. Soil and plant scientists working for the federal government earned mean salaries of $67,530 a year in 2006. Botanists who have advanced training and experience can earn more than $90,000 annually. Benefits vary but usually include paid holidays and vacations, and health insurance.

WORK ENVIRONMENT

Botanists work in a wide variety of settings, some of them very pleasant: greenhouses, botanical gardens, and herbariums, for example. A botanist working for an environmental consultant or conservation organization may spend a lot of time outdoors, rain or shine. Some botanists interact with the public, such as in a public park or greenhouse, sharing their enthusiasm for the field. Other botanists spend their days in a lab, poring over specimens and writing up the results of their research.

As scientists, botanists need to be focused, patient, and determined. A botanist needs to believe in what he or she is doing and keep at a project until it's completed satisfactorily. The ability to work on one's own is important, but few scientists work in a vacuum. They cooperate with others, share the results of their work orally and in writing, and, particularly in private industry, may need to explain what they're doing in layman's terms.

Some research spans many hours and even years of work. At times, research botanists deeply involved with a project put in a lot of overtime. In exchange, they may be able to work fewer hours other weeks, depending on the specific employer. Botanists performing fieldwork also might have some flexibility of hours. In private industry, the workweek is likely to be a standard 35 to 40 hours.

Educational requirements for botanists are high and so much of the work involves research. Therefore it is important to be a good scholar and enjoy digging for answers.

OUTLOOK

Employment for all biological scientists, including botanists, is expected to grow about as fast as the average for all occupations through 2014, according to the U.S. Department of Labor. Botanists will be needed to help meet growing environmental, conservation, pharmaceutical, and similar demands. However, budget cuts and a large number of graduates have made competition for jobs strong. Government employment opportunities should stay strong, but will depend in part on the continued health of the national economy.

Federal budget cuts may jeopardize some projects and positions. Experts say the outlook is best for those with an advanced degree.

FOR MORE INFORMATION

For the booklets Careers in Botany *and* Botany for the Next Millennium, *contact*
Botanical Society of America
PO Box 299
St. Louis, MO 63166-0299
Tel: 314-577-9566
Email: bsa-manager@botany.org
http://www.botany.org

For information about internships with state chapters or at TNC headquarters, contact
The Nature Conservancy (TNC)
4245 North Fairfax Drive, Suite 100
Arlington, VA 22203-1606
Tel: 800-628-6860
http://www.nature.org

To learn about volunteer positions in natural resource management, contact
Student Conservation Association
689 River Road
PO Box 550
Charlestown, NH 03603-0550
Tel: 603-543-1700
http://www.thesca.org

This government agency manages more than 540 national wildlife refuges. The service's Web site has information on volunteer opportunities, careers, and answers to frequently asked questions.
U.S. Fish & Wildlife Service
U.S. Department of the Interior
1849 C Street, NW
Washington, DC 20240-0001
Tel: 800-344-9453
Email: contact@fws.gov
http://www.fws.gov

Enologists

OVERVIEW

Enologists, or *winemakers,* direct and manage most activities of a winery, including planting grapes and producing, storing, and shipping wine. They select the type of grapes grown and supervise workers in the production process from harvesting to fermenting, aging, and bottling. Enologists work with different varieties of grapes in a type or species to develop the strongest and most flavorful wines.

HISTORY

Winemaking has been practiced for more than 5,000 years. Ancient Egyptians had hieroglyphics representing wine making, and it was an important commodity in Palestine during the time of Jesus. The Chinese made wine more than 4,000 years ago, as did the Greeks and Romans.

Throughout history, wine has been used as a drink to accompany meals or as part of religious practices. In fact, the use of wine spread throughout Europe because of its use in religious services. Wine also was used as a medicine or curative.

Grapes have been cultivated in the United States since the late 1700s. Enology or viticulture, the cultivation of grapes, is a major industry now, primarily in California, the Pacific Northwest and the Northeast. Approximately 95 percent of the U.S. domestic wine is cultivated in California. Enologists have played an instrumental role in the growth of the wine industry, experimenting with different types of grapes and growing conditions and improving the quality of wines produced.

THE JOB

Enologists are involved in all aspects of wine production and therefore must have a thorough knowledge of the winemaking business. They must be able to analyze the quality of grapes, decide which vines are best to grow, determine when grapes are ripe enough to be picked, and coordinate the process of wine making. Production decisions include which yeast or bacteria to use, at what temperature fermentation should occur, and how the wine should be aged.

Selection of the proper grapes is a vital part of an enologist's planning responsibilities. This selection process includes analyzing the varieties of grapes to determine which are best suited to grow in a specific area, given existing soil and climate conditions. For example, an enologist in California must ensure that grapes chosen to grow in that climate can withstand the heat of the summers, while an enologist in New York must ensure that grapes chosen can withstand the cooler temperatures there. Other factors that determine which type of grapes to grow include the desired flavor and aroma of wines and the species' ability to withstand disease.

Grapes that produce red wine are processed in a different way than grapes that produce white wine. Production methods also vary according to the size of the winery and the type of containers and stainless steel tanks used in the crushing and fermentation processes. Enologists have the final word in all of the production decisions. They consult with other winery staff about issues involving the testing and crushing of grapes, the cooling, filtering, and bottling of the wine, and the type of storage casks in which to place the wine. The enologist also researches and implements modifications in growing and production techniques to ensure the best quality product at the lowest cost. This involves keeping up with technological improvements in production methods and the ability to read and analyze a profit-and-loss statement and other parts of a balance sheet.

Enologists oversee personnel matters. They may hire and train employees such as vineyard and production workers, coordinate work schedules, and develop a salary structure. Good communication skills are needed to present written and oral reports.

Although bookkeeping, reporting to government agencies, and other administrative tasks often are delegated to an assistant, enologists must have an understanding of industry regulations, accounting, and mathematics. Production costs and other expenses must be carefully recorded. Because of the increased use of computers for recording composition and grape details, blending and production alternatives, and analyzing information, enologists should have some training in computer science.

An enologist tests a wine sample. *(Jeff Greenberg, The Image Works)*

An enologist sometimes is involved with decisions regarding the marketing of the finished product. Production, transportation, and distribution costs, the potential markets on the national and international level, and other factors must be calculated to determine the price of the finished wine and where the wine will be sold.

REQUIREMENTS

High School
In high school, you should take courses in mathematics, biology, chemistry, and physics. You should also take English and other courses that enhance communications skills. Foreign languages, particularly French and German, may enhance opportunities for study or research abroad.

Postsecondary Training
Although some wineries offer on-the-job training in the form of apprenticeships for high school graduates, the majority of entry-level positions go to college graduates.

A bachelor's degree in enology or viticulture is preferred, but a degree in food or fermentation science or a related subject such as microbiology or biochemistry is acceptable. Specific courses related to winery management should include wine analysis and wine microbiology. Business, economics, marketing, and computer science should also be part of the degree program. There are enology programs at the University of California–Davis, California State University–Fresno, the University of Washington, the University of Arkansas, Oregon State University, and Cornell University. Washington State University Tri-Cities offers a bachelor of science degree in agriculture with emphasis in viticulture and enology. Associate's degrees in enology and related areas are available at Walla Walla Community College, Chemeketa Community College, and other schools.

As competition in the field increases, many enologists are choosing to pursue a master's degree and to gain experience in related scientific research.

Although no licenses or certificates are necessary to work in the field, many enologists choose to continue professional enrichment through continuing education classes and affiliation with organizations such as the American Society for Enology and Viticulture.

Other Requirements
Enologists need excellent verbal and written communication skills, and you must be able to handle multiple tasks and priorities. You

must take direction from supervisors and work well on a team. Basic computer knowledge is important, as is familiarity with the Bureau of Alcohol, Tobacco, Firearms, and Explosives and state regulations concerning wine making, handling, and transport.

Enologists must be familiar with safety equipment and procedures. You need the physical strength to climb stairs, work on high platforms, lift and carry 40 pounds, bend, squat, and stretch. Most wineries require you to be at least 21 years of age.

EXPLORING

Part-time or summer employment at a winery is an excellent method of gaining an insight into the skills and temperament needed for this profession. A high school student also can explore opportunities in the field through discussions with professionals already working as enologists. Because many technical colleges offer evening courses, it may be possible for a high school student to audit or take a course for future college credit.

EMPLOYERS

Enologists are employed in a variety of settings, from small wineries to large manufacturing plants and multinational corporations. Some enologists may do research or quality assurance work. Since many vineyards and wineries are located in California, jobs are more abundant there.

STARTING OUT

The usual method of entry is to be hired by a winery after completing an undergraduate or graduate degree in enology, fermentation, or food science. Summer or part-time work sometimes may lead to a permanent job, and an apprenticeship program at the winery provides the necessary training.

ADVANCEMENT

Advancement depends on performance, experience, and education. Enologists at small wineries may become managers at larger facilities. Those at larger facilities may move on to direct a number of wineries as part of a nationwide organization. A small number of enologists may start their own wineries. Because of the relatively small number of wineries in the country and the fact that enologists have high-level management positions from the start, advancement opportunities are somewhat limited.

EARNINGS

A survey of the wine industry by *Wine Business Monthly* in 2006 reports that salaries ranged from a low of $20,030 for unskilled workers in the cellar or tasting room to highs of more than $585,000 for top winemakers and other executives at some larger wineries. Assistant winemaker is a typical position for an enology graduate with a few years experience. Median salaries in this position ranged from $60,414 at small wineries to $65,028 at large wineries. Salaries listed for enologists ranged from $31,200 to $68,026, depending on the size of the establishment. Earnings for vineyard managers ranged from $36,000 to $115,000, depending on vineyard size. Median annual salaries for the president of a winery ranged from $133,167 for those producing under 50,000 cases per year to $243,231 for those which produced over 500,000 cases a year.

WORK ENVIRONMENT

Enologists work mostly indoors, with some outdoor activities in a vineyard. Enologists enjoy variety in their jobs as they constantly alternate between analyzing the grapes in the field, assessing the development of wines, studying current production techniques, planning marketing strategies for the upcoming harvest, and other responsibilities. Physical labor such as lifting a 40-pound wine case or pruning a vineyard may be required.

During most of the year an enologist works 40 hours a week, but during the late summer and early fall when the grape harvest occurs, an enologist should expect to work long hours six or seven days a week for a four- to six-week period.

As a manager, an enologist should be able to communicate and work well with people. The ability to interpret data is vital as much of the enologist's planning responsibilities involve working with crop and market forecasts. Attention to detail is critical. An enologist should be able to spend long hours analyzing information and make and implement decisions concerning this information.

OUTLOOK

Job growth is tied to the size and quality of grape harvests, the success of wine production, and the foreign and domestic demand for American wines. Technological advances in wine production may create more job opportunities. Over the past decade, U.S. wine exports increased from $196 million in 1994 to $876 million in 2006, according to the U.S. Department of Commerce.

However, it is impossible to predict weather and soil conditions from season to season and there is little security, especially for smaller wine producers. There is stiff competition in the wine business and there have been a number of consolidations and mergers in the past few years. Still, new brands continue to be introduced with strong marketing campaigns, particularly in the lower and mid-priced categories.

Job opportunities will be best in California, where most of the U.S. wineries are located. Most California wine is cultivated in the San Joaquin, Napa, and Sonoma valleys, the central coast, and the Sierra foothills. But with wineries now located in all 50 states and the District of Columbia, it is possible to find employment opportunities outside of California.

FOR MORE INFORMATION

For information on various aspects of winemaking, contact
American Society for Enology and Viticulture
PO Box 1855
Davis, CA 95617-1855
Tel: 530-753-3142
http://www.asev.org

For information on education and chapter events, including competitions and wine tastings, contact
American Wine Society
113 South Perry Street
Lawrenceville, GA 30045-4811
Tel: 678-377-7070
http://www.americanwinesociety.com

Farm Crop Production Technicians

OVERVIEW

Farm crop production technicians are involved with farmers and agricultural businesses in all aspects of planting, growing, and marketing crops. With backgrounds in agriculture and scientific research, they advise farmers on the best techniques to produce crops. They may also work for companies that produce agricultural products such as fertilizer and equipment to make sure they are meeting the needs of farmers.

HISTORY

Until the early 20th century, crops were planted, maintained, and harvested by individual farmers. During harvest, farmers may have called upon the assistance of neighboring farmers or local work crews, but most aspects of crop production were handled by family members. The typical family farm measured about 160 acres. Horses were used to power simple machinery that was repaired, and often built, by the farmers themselves. Although the family farm once stood as a symbol of independent living, the demands of agricultural production throughout the 20th century called upon the skills, talents, and labors of others.

Advances in equipment technology, methods of conservation, and pesticides and fertilizers led to more farm output, but also resulted in fewer family farms. By 1950, the average farm had grown greatly in size and needed to be highly efficient in order to turn a profit. Farm owners began to rely on outside assistance in crop production, and those with farm experience, but without their own farms, found new career opportunities in crop production assistance. Agribusiness developed in the 1960s to help farmers with the complicated process of managing a farm crop, from the selecting of seed to the marketing of the final product. Today, technicians, engineers, scientists, conservationists, and government agencies work together to help farms stay profitable and produce crops for a global market.

THE JOB

Corn, soybeans, wheat, cotton, fruit—these are some of the top crops in the agricultural industry. The farms and orchards that produce these crops have very specific needs, differing from the needs of livestock and dairy farms. Farm crop production technicians understand how to best prepare soil, treat plants, and harvest crops. These technicians may have different employers, from scientists to government agencies to the farmers themselves, but they share intentions—to use their knowledge of crops and production to help farmers increase yields and market their products. And the work can be varied, involving grading and handling, pest and disease control, finding new uses for crops, and other tasks.

Nearly everything used on a farm is now purchased from outside suppliers: seed, fertilizer, pesticides, machinery, fuels, and general supplies. Companies selling these products need farm-trained technicians who understand buyers' farming problems and needs. Farm supply companies also need technicians to assist in research and development. These technicians work under the supervision of feed or chemical company scientists, carrying out the details of the testing program.

In the production phase of crop technology, some technicians make soil or tissue tests to determine the efficiency of fertilizer programs. Others are responsible for the maintenance of farm machinery. More experienced farm crop production technicians may oversee the complete management of a farm, including personnel, machinery, and finances.

Most agricultural products need some processing before they reach the consumer. Processing involves testing, grading, packaging, and transporting. Some of the technicians in this area work closely with farmers and need to know a great deal about crop production. For example, *field-contact technicians* employed by food-processing companies monitor crop production on the farms from which the companies buy products. In some processing companies, technicians supervise the entire crop operation. In others, they act as buyers or determine when crops will be harvested for processing and shipping.

Some technicians may work for the government or businesses performing quality-control work or nutrition research; others work as inspectors. This work is usually done in a laboratory.

In addition to the positions mentioned above, farm crop production technicians may take on the following titles and responsibilities.

Processing and distributing technicians may find jobs with canneries, freezing and packing plants, cooperatives, or distributors to make sure the work is up to government standards and to advise on matters of efficiency and profitability. They may work either in the laboratory or in the field with the grower. *Laboratory technicians* work with scientists to maintain quality control, test, grade, measure, and keep records. *Field technicians* supervise seed selection and planting, weed and pest control, irrigation, harvesting, and on-the-spot testing to ensure that crops are harvested at precisely the right state of maturity.

Seed production field supervisors help coordinate the activities of farmers who produce seed for commercial seed companies. They inspect and analyze soil and water supplies for farms and study other growing conditions in order to plan production of planted crops. They distribute seed stock to farmers, specify areas and numbers of acres to be planted, and give instructions to workers engaged in cultivation procedures, such as fertilization, tilling, and detasseling. They may also determine dates and methods for harvesting, storing, and shipping seed crops.

Biological aides assist research workers in biology, bacteriology, plant pathology, mycology, and related agricultural sciences. They set up laboratory and field equipment, perform routine tests, and clean up and maintain field and laboratory equipment. They also keep records of plant growth, experimental plots, greenhouse activity, insecticide use, and other agricultural experimentation.

Spray equipment operators work for pest-control companies. They select and apply the proper herbicides or pesticides for particular jobs, formulate mixtures, and operate various types of spraying and dusting equipment. A specialized technician within this occupation is the *aircraft crop duster* or *sprayer*.

REQUIREMENTS

High School

You should take courses in mathematics and science; depending on your area of work, you'll need an understanding of biology and chemistry. You should complete as much vocational agriculture work as possible, including agricultural mechanics. In addition, English is very important, because much of the work requires good communication skills.

Postsecondary Training

A career as a farm crop production technician requires training in a rigorous two-year technical or agricultural college program in order to learn the principles of crop production. In such a training program, you can expect to take a broad range of courses relating to agriculture in general and farm crop production in particular, as well as some general education courses. Typical first-year courses include the following: agricultural machinery, animal husbandry, soil science, entomology, English, physical education, science, and mathematics. Typical second-year courses include agricultural economics, soil fertility, plant pathology, forage and seed crops, and social science.

If you wish to specialize in vegetable or fruit production, you may be able to modify your program to concentrate in these areas. You may study topics such as vegetable and fruit production in the first year and vegetable and fruit marketing in the second.

Certification or Licensing

The majority of technicians in the field are not required to have a license or certification. However, technicians involved in grading or inspecting for local, state, or federal government units must pass examinations to be qualified. Some other government jobs, such as that of research assistant, may also require a competitive examination.

Other Requirements

You'll need manual skills and mechanical ability to operate various kinds of equipment and machinery. You must also be able to apply scientific principles to the processing procedures, materials, and measuring and control devices found at the modern laboratory or farm. You must be able to communicate what needs to be done and interpret the orders you are given.

EXPLORING

Students who grow up on farms have the best opportunity to explore this field, but living on a farm is not the only way to check out this work. You can also join the local branch of the National FFA Organization (formerly Future Farmers of America) or a local 4-H club. These groups will give you the opportunity to work on farm projects and meet professionals in the field. You may also be able to obtain work experience on farms during the summer when extra labor is always required for planting, detasseling, and harvesting. During postsecondary training, heavy emphasis is placed on supervised occupational experience.

If you are between the ages of five and 22, you might also want to join the National Junior Horticulture Association, which offers horticulture-related projects, contests, and other activities. Visit http://www.njha.org for more information.

EMPLOYERS

With a background in crop production, the farm crop production technician is able to find work in a variety of settings. Although some may work directly for farmers, most of these technicians work in businesses that support agriculture. They can work for feed and supply companies, inspection departments and other government agencies, nurseries, grain elevators, and farm equipment sales and service companies. They work under the supervision of agricultural scientists, farm managers, and agribusiness professionals.

STARTING OUT

Once you are in a postsecondary training program, you will be encouraged to decide as early as possible which phase of crop technology you prefer to enter, because contacts made while in school can be helpful in obtaining a job after the program's completion. You will find that students are often hired by the same firm they worked for during a work-study program. If that firm does not have a position open, a recommendation from the employer will help with other firms.

Most faculty members in a technical program have contact with prospective employers and can help place qualified students. You can also take advantage of your school's placement service, which should arrange interviews between students and prospective employers.

ADVANCEMENT

Technicians in the field of farm crop production have many opportunities for advancement. Early advancement will be easier for those who combine a formal technical education with work experience. Those who have had several jobs in the industry will probably advance to managerial levels more rapidly than those who have not. As more postsecondary schools are established in local communities, it becomes easier for employed persons to continue their education through evening classes while they work. Although a bachelor's degree in agriculture may be required to advance to some positions, technicians may be able to substitute a great deal of experience for the degree. Some technicians are able to become managers, supervisors, sales representatives, and agribusiness or farm owners.

EARNINGS

Salaries of farm crop production technicians vary widely. Technicians employed in off-the-farm jobs often receive higher salaries than technicians working on farms. Salaries are influenced by such factors as the technician's educational background, the geographic area he or she is employed in, the technician's agricultural experience, and the type of crop involved.

The *Career Guide to Industries* reports that the median weekly earnings for all workers in agricultural production were $417 in 2004 ($21,654 annually for full-time work), with a range of less $248 a week (or $12,896 a year) for the lowest paid 10 percent, to more than $915 a week ($47,580 a year) for the highest paid 10 percent. Median hourly earnings for farmworkers in crops, nurseries, and greenhouses were $7.95 ($16,540 for full-time work annually) in 2006. In 2006, farm and home management advisers earned salaries that ranged from less than $21,560 to more than $73,520, with a median salary of $41,710. Biological technicians earned median annual salaries of $35,710 in 2006, according to the U.S. Department of Labor.

Technicians working on farms, however, often receive food and housing benefits that can be the equivalent of several thousand dollars a year. Health coverage and other benefits also depend on the position and employer.

WORK ENVIRONMENT

Certain technicians in this field work primarily outdoors and must be able to adapt to extreme weather conditions. There may be certain seasons of the year when they are required to work long hours under considerable pressure to get a crop harvested or processed at just the right time.

The work of laboratory technicians in this field involves exacting systematic procedures in facilities that are generally clean and comfortable. Work in the processing phase is usually indoors, except for the field-service or field-contact personnel, who spend much of their time outdoors.

Planting a new field, orchard, or vineyard, and watching it grow and develop, can be extremely rewarding. However, a stable temperament is essential when facing the continual uncertainties of weather conditions, such as possible blight or premature frost, which may mean the possible loss of one's investment.

For technicians who feel they may lack some of these characteristics, employment in sales and services is advised. Here, too, on-the-job satisfaction can be found playing a vital role in producing humanity's most basic need.

OUTLOOK

While farm products have not decreased in importance, the employment of farmers and farm managers today is on the decline as farms consolidate and become more mechanized. The U.S. Department of Labor predicts that employment for farm workers involved in food and fiber crop production will also decline through 2014. However, workers will be needed to replace those who leave the field, and organizations, such as the Peace Corps, can provide opportunities for agricultural technicians in the underdeveloped nations of the world.

For technicians interested specifically in orchard and vineyard production, the outlook may be somewhat brighter. Those technicians hoping to own or operate their own orchards or vineyards should remember, of course, that not all crops are necessarily good investments at all times. Local conditions, business cycles, and supply and demand must be considered when making decisions on the planting of a certain kind of orchard, grove, or vineyard.

FOR MORE INFORMATION

For information on agricultural careers, contact
American Society of Agronomy
677 South Segoe Road
Madison, WI 53711-1086

Tel: 608-273-8080
Email: headquarters@agronomy.org
http://www.agronomy.org

To read about research projects concerning crop production, visit the USDA Web site, or contact
U.S. Department of Agriculture (USDA)
1400 Independence Avenue, SW
Washington, DC 20250-0002
Tel: 202-720-2791
http://www.usda.gov

Farmers

School Subjects
Agriculture
Business
Earth science

Personal Skills
Leadership/management
Mechanical/manipulative

Work Environment
Primarily outdoors
Primarily multiple locations

Minimum Education Level
High school diploma

Salary Range
$22,750 to $37,130 to
$100,050+

Certification or Licensing
Voluntary

Outlook
Decline

DOT
421

GOE
03.01.01

NOC
8251

O*NET-SOC
11-9011.00, 11-9011.02,
11-9012.00, 45-1011.00

OVERVIEW

Farmers either own or lease land on which they raise crops, such as corn, wheat, tobacco, cotton, vegetables, or fruits; raise animals or poultry; or maintain herds of dairy cattle for the production of milk. Whereas some farmers may combine several of these activities, most specialize in one specific area. They are assisted by *farm laborers*—either hired workers or members of farm families—who perform various tasks.

As increasingly complex technology continues to impact the agricultural industry, farms are becoming larger. Most contemporary farms are thousands of acres in size and include massive animal and plant production operations. Subsistence farms, which produce only enough to support the farmer's family, are becoming increasingly rare. There are nearly 1.3 million farmers employed in the United States.

HISTORY

In colonial America, almost 95 percent of the population were farmers, planting such crops as corn, wheat, flax, and, further south, tobacco. Livestock including hogs, cattle, sheep, and goats were imported from Europe. Farmers raised hay to feed livestock and often just enough other crops to supply their families with a balanced diet throughout the year. Progress in science and technology in the 18th and 19th centuries allowed for societies to develop in different directions, and to build other industries, but over one-half of the world's population is still engaged in farming today.

In the early 20th century, farmers raised a variety of crops along with cattle, poultry, and dairy cows. Farm labor was handled by the farmers and their families. Farmers were very self-sufficient, living on their farms and maintaining their own equipment and

A farmer (right) and a district conservationist discuss ways to improve crop yield while conserving natural resources. *(Ken Hammond, Natural Resources Conservation Service)*

storage. Between 1910 and 1960, when horsepower was replaced by mechanized equipment, about 90 million acres previously devoted to growing hay for the feeding of horses could be planted with other crops. Advances in farming techniques and production led to larger farms and more specialization by farmers. Farmers began to focus on growing one or two crops. About this time, more tenant farmers entered the business, renting land for cash or a share of the crops.

Farmers doubled their output between 1950 and 1980, but there were fewer of them. In that time, the farm population decreased from 23 million to 6 million. After 1980, many farmers began supplementing their household income with off-farm jobs and businesses.

Today, some small-scale farmers are finding success by catering to niche markets such as organic foods and specialty crops. Others are even branching off into aquaculture—the commercial farming of fish.

THE JOB

There are probably as many different types of farmers as there are different types of plants and animals whose products are consumed by humans. In addition to *diversified crops farmers*, who grow different combinations of fruits, grains, and vegetables, and *general farmers*, who raise livestock as well as crops, there are *cash grain farmers*, who grow barley, corn, rice, soybeans, and wheat; *vegetable farmers*; *tree-fruit-and-nut crops farmers*; *field crops farmers*, who raise alfalfa, cotton, hops, peanuts, mint, sugarcane, and tobacco; *animal breeders*; *fur farmers*; *livestock ranchers*; *dairy farmers*; *poultry farmers*; *beekeepers*; *reptile farmers*; *fish farmers*; and even *worm growers*.

In addition to the different types of crop farmers, there are two different types of farming management careers: the *farm operator* and the *farm manager*.

The farm operator either owns his or her own farm or leases land from other farms. Farm operators' responsibilities vary depending on the type of farm they run, but in general they are responsible for making managerial decisions. They determine the best time to seed, fertilize, cultivate, spray, and harvest. They keep extensive financial and inventory records of the farm operations, which are now done with the help of computer programs.

Farm operators perform tasks ranging from caring for livestock to erecting sheds. The size of the farm often determines what tasks the operators handle themselves. On very large farms, operators hire employees to perform tasks that operators on small farms would do themselves.

The farm manager has a wide range of duties. The owner of a large livestock farm may hire a farm manager to oversee a single activity, such as feeding the livestock. In other cases, a farm manager may oversee the entire operation of a small farm for an absentee owner. Farm management firms often employ highly skilled farm managers to manage specific operations on a small farm or to oversee tenant farm operations on several farms.

Whether farm operators or managers, the farmers' duties vary widely depending on what product they farm. A common type of farmer is the *crop farmer*. Following are a number of crops that a crop farmer might manage.

Corn farmers and wheat farmers begin the growing season by breaking up the soil with plows, then harrowing, pulverizing, and leveling it. Some of these tasks may be done after the harvest the previous year and others just before planting. Corn is usually planted around the middle of May with machines that place the corn seeds into dirt hills a few inches apart, making weed control easier. On the average, a crop is cultivated three times during a season. Corn is also used in the making of silage, a type of animal feed made by cutting the corn and allowing it to ferment in storage silos.

Wheat may be sown in the fall or spring, depending on the severity of the past winter and the variety of wheat being sown. Wheat is planted with a drill, close together, allowing greater cultivation and easier harvesting. The harvest for winter wheat occurs in early summer. Wheat farmers use machines called combines to gather and thresh the wheat in one operation. The wheat is then stored in large grain storage elevators, which are owned by private individuals, companies, or farming cooperatives.

Cotton and tobacco planting begins in March in the Southwest and somewhat later in the Southeast. Tobacco plants must be carefully protected from harsh weather conditions. The soil in which tobacco is grown must be thoroughly broken up, smoothed, and fertilized before planting, as tobacco is very hard on the soil.

The peanut crop can be managed like other types of farm crops. It is not especially sensitive to weather and disease, nor does it require the great care of tobacco and cotton.

Specialty crops such as fruits and vegetables are subject to seasonal variations, so the farmer usually relies heavily on hired seasonal labor. This type of farmer uses more specialized equipment than do general farmers.

The mechanization of farming has not eliminated all the problems of raising crops. Judgment and experience are always important in making decisions. The hay farmer, for example, must determine the time for mowing that will yield the best crop in terms of stem toughness and leaf loss. These decisions must be weighed against possible harsh weather conditions. To harvest hay, hay farmers use specialized equipment such as mowing machines and hay rakes that are usually drawn by tractors. The hay is pressed into bales by another machine for easier storage and then transported to storage facilities or to market.

Decisions about planting are just as crucial as those about harvesting. For example, potatoes need to be planted during a relatively short span of days in the spring. The fields must be tilled and ready for planting, and the farmer must estimate weather conditions so the seedlings will not freeze from late winter weather.

The specialty crop farmer uses elaborate irrigation systems to water crops during seasons of inadequate rainfall. Often these systems are portable, as it is necessary to move the equipment from field to field.

Farms are strongly influenced by the weather, crop diseases, fluctuations in prices of domestic and foreign farm products, and, in some cases, federal farm programs. Farmers must carefully plan the combination of crops they will grow so that if the price of one crop drops they will have sufficient income from another to make up for it. Since prices change from month to month, farmers who plan ahead may be able to store their crops or keep their livestock to take advantage of better prices later in the year.

Farmers who raise and breed animals for milk or meat are called livestock and cattle farmers. There are various types of farmers that fall into this category.

Livestock farmers generally buy calves from ranchers who breed and raise them. They feed and fatten young cattle and often raise their own corn and hay to lower feeding costs. They need to be familiar with cattle diseases and proper methods of feeding. They provide their cattle with fenced pasturage and adequate shelter from rough weather. Some livestock farmers specialize in breeding stock for sale to ranchers and dairy farmers. These specialists maintain and improve purebred animals of a particular breed. Bulls and cows are then sold to ranchers and dairy farmers who want to improve their herds.

Sheep ranchers raise sheep primarily for their wool. Large herds are maintained on rangeland in the western states. Since large areas of land are needed, the sheep rancher must usually buy grazing rights on government-owned lands.

Although *dairy farmers'* first concern is the production of high-grade milk, they also raise corn and grain to provide feed for their animals. Dairy farmers must be able to repair the many kinds of equipment essential to their business and know about diseases, sanitation, and methods of improving the quantity and quality of the milk.

Dairy animals must be milked twice every day, once in the morning and once at night. Records are kept of each cow's production of milk to ascertain which cows are profitable and which should be traded or sold for meat. After milking, when the cows are at pasture, the farmer cleans the stalls and barn by washing, sweeping, and sterilizing milking equipment with boiling water. This is extremely important because dairy cows easily contract diseases from unsanitary conditions, and this in turn may contaminate the milk. Dairy farmers must have their herds certified to be free of disease by the U.S. Department of Health and Human Services.

The great majority of *poultry farmers* do not hatch their own chicks but buy them from commercial hatcheries. The chicks are kept in brooder houses until they are seven or eight weeks old and are then transferred to open pens or shelters. After six months, the hens begin to lay eggs, and roosters are culled from the flock to be sold for meat.

The primary duty of poultry farmers is to keep their flocks healthy. They provide shelter from the chickens' natural enemies and from extreme weather conditions. The shelters are kept extremely clean, because diseases can spread through a flock rapidly. The poultry farmer selects the food that best allows each chicken to grow or produce to its greatest potential while at the same time keeping costs down.

Raising chickens to be sold as broilers or fryers requires equipment to house them until they are six to 13 weeks old. Farmers specializing in the production of eggs gather eggs at least twice a day and more often in very warm weather. The eggs then are stored in a cool place, inspected, graded, and packed for market. The poultry farmer who specializes in producing broilers is usually not an independent producer but is under contract with a backer, who is often the operator of a slaughterhouse or the manufacturer of poultry feeds.

Beekeepers set up and manage beehives and harvest and sell the excess honey that bees don't use as their own food. The sale of honey is less profitable than the business of cultivating bees for lease to farmers to help pollinate their crops.

Farmers and farm managers make a wide range of administrative decisions. In addition to their knowledge of crop production

U.S. Farm Facts

Total farmland: 938.28 million acres

Percentage of total U.S. land area: 41 percent

Number of certified organic farms: 11,998

Average farm size: 441 acres

Average age of farm operators: 55.3 years

Gender of farm operators: Male: 72.8 percent; Female: 27.2 percent

Percentage of farmers who use the Internet for farm business: 39 percent

Top five agricultural commodities: Cattle and calves, dairy products, corn, broilers, and soybeans

Top agricultural counties (by financial value): Fresno County, California; Tulare County, California; Monterey County, California

Top poultry and egg-producing counties (by financial value): Sussex County, Delaware; Rockingham County, Virginia; Benton County, Arkansas

Top berry-producing counties (by number of acres): Washington County, Maine; Monterey County, California; Plymouth County, Massachusetts

Source: 2002 Census of Agriculture, U.S. Department of Agriculture

and animal science, they determine how to market the foods they produce. They keep an eye on the commodities markets to see which crops are most profitable. They take out loans to buy farm equipment or additional land for cultivation. They keep up with new methods of production and new markets. Farms today are large, complex businesses, complete with the requisite anxiety over cash flow, competition, markets, and production.

REQUIREMENTS

High School

Take classes in math, accounting, and business to prepare for the management responsibilities of running a farm. To further assist you in management, take computer classes. Chemistry, biology, and earth science classes can help you understand the various processes of crop production. Technical and shop courses will help you to better understand agricultural machinery. With county extension courses, you can keep abreast of developments in farm technology.

Postsecondary Training

Although there are no specific educational requirements for this field, every successful farmer, whether working with crops or animals, must know the principles of soil preparation and cultivation, disease control, and machinery maintenance, as well as a mastery of business practices and bookkeeping. Farmers must know their crops well enough to be able to choose the proper seeds for their particular soil and climate. They also need experience in evaluating crop growth and weather cycles. Livestock and dairy farmers should enjoy working with animals and have some background in animal science, breeding, and care.

The state land-grant universities across the country were established to encourage agricultural research and to educate young people in the latest advancements in farming. They offer agricultural programs that award bachelor's degrees as well as shorter programs in specific areas. Some universities offer advanced studies in horticulture, animal science, agronomy, and agricultural economics. Most students in agricultural colleges are also required to take courses in farm management, business, finance, and economics. Two-year colleges often have programs leading to associate's degrees in agriculture.

Certification or Licensing

The American Society of Farm Managers and Rural Appraisers offers farm operators voluntary certification as an accredited farm manager. Certification requires five years' experience working on a farm, an academic background—a bachelor's or preferably a master's degree in a branch of agricultural science—and courses covering the business, financial, and legal aspects of farm management.

Other Requirements

You'll need to keep up to date on new farming methods throughout the world. You must be flexible and innovative enough to adapt to new technologies that will produce crops or raise livestock more efficiently. You should also have good mechanical aptitude and be able to work with a wide variety of tools and machinery.

EXPLORING

Most people who become farmers have grown up on farms; if your family doesn't own a farm, there are opportunities for part-time work as a hired hand, especially during seasonal operations. If you live in an agricultural community, you should be able to find work as a detasseler in the summer time. Although the work is hot and strenuous, it will quickly familiarize you with aspects of crop production and the hard work it takes to operate a farm.

In addition, organizations such as the National 4-H Council (http://www.fourhcouncil.edu) and the National FFA Organization (http://www.ffa.org) offer good opportunities for learning about, visiting, and participating in farming activities. Agricultural colleges often have their own farms where students can gain actual experience in farm operations in addition to classroom work.

If you are between the ages of five and 22, you might also want to join the National Junior Horticulture Association, which offers horticulture-related projects, contests, and other activities. Visit http://www.njha.org for more information.

EMPLOYERS

Nearly 1.3 million farmers are employed in the United States. About 83 percent of farmers are self-employed, working on land they've inherited, purchased, or leased. Those who don't own land, but who have farming experience, may find work on large commercial farms or with agricultural supply companies as consultants or managers. Farmers with seasonal crops may work for agriculture-related businesses during the off-season or may work temporarily as farm hands for livestock farms and ranches. They may also own other businesses, such as farm equipment sales and service.

STARTING OUT

It is becoming increasingly difficult for a person to purchase land for farming. The capital investment in a farm today is so great that it is almost impossible for anyone to start from scratch. However, those who lack a family connection to farming or who do not have enough money to start their own farm can lease land from other farmers. Money for leasing land and equipment may be available from local banks or the Farm Service Agency.

Because the capital outlay is so high, many wheat, corn, and specialty crop farmers often start as *tenant farmers*, renting land and equipment. They may also share the cash profits with the owner of the land. In this way, these tenants hope to gain both the experience and cash to purchase and manage their own farms.

Livestock farmers generally start by renting property and sometimes animals on a share-of-the-profits basis with the owner. Government lands, such as national parks, can be rented for pasture as well. Later, when the livestock farmer wants to own property, it is possible to borrow based on the estimated value of the leased land, buildings, and animals. Dairy farmers can begin in much the same way. However, loans are becoming more difficult to obtain. After several years of lenient loan policies, financial institutions in farm regions have tightened their requirements.

ADVANCEMENT

Farmers advance by buying their own farms or additional acreage to increase production and income. With a farm's success, a farmer can also invest in better equipment and technology and can hire managers and workers to attend to much of the farm's operation. This is true for crop, livestock, dairy, or poultry farmers. In farming, as in other fields, a person's success depends greatly on education, motivation, and keeping up with the latest developments.

EARNINGS

Farmers' incomes vary greatly from year to year, since the prices of farm products fluctuate according to weather conditions and the amount and quality of what all farmers were able to produce. A farm that shows a large profit one year may show a loss for the following year. Most farmers, especially those running small farms, earn incomes from nonfarm activities that are several times larger than their farm incomes. Farm incomes also vary greatly depending on the size and type of farm. In general, large farms generate more income than small farms. Exceptions include some specialty farms that produce low-volume but high-quality horticultural and fruit products.

The Economic Research Service (ERS) of the U.S. Department of Agriculture reports that the average farm household income was $83,660 in 2005. This income, it is important to note, includes earnings from off-farm jobs, businesses, and other sources. Farm managers who worked full time had median annual earnings of $52,070 in 2006, according to the U.S. Department of Labor. The lowest paid 10 percent of farm managers earned less than $29,760 a year, and the top 10 percent of all farm managers earned $100,050 or more a year. Farmers and ranchers earned salaries that ranged from less than $22,750 to more than $76,030 in 2006, with a median of $37,130.

WORK ENVIRONMENT

The farmer's daily life has its rewards and dangers. Machine-related injuries, exposure to the weather, and illnesses caused by allergies or animal-related diseases are just some of the hazards that farmers face on a regular basis. In addition, farms are often isolated, away from many conveniences and necessities, such as immediate medical attention.

Farming can be a difficult and frustrating career, but for many it is a satisfying way of life. The hours are long and the work is physically strenuous, but working outdoors and watching the fruits of one's labor grow before one's eyes can be very rewarding. The changing seasons bring variety to the day-to-day work. Farmers seldom work five eight-hour days a week. When harvesting time comes or the weather is right for planting or spraying, farmers work long hours to see that everything gets done. Even during the cold winter months they stay busy repairing machinery and buildings. Dairy farmers and other livestock farmers work seven days a week year round.

OUTLOOK

Employment of farmers and ranchers is expected to decline through 2014, according to the U.S. Department of Labor. The department predicts that employment for farm and ranch managers will grow more slowly than the average during that same time span. Every year can be different for farmers, as production, expansion, and markets are affected by weather, exports, and other factors. Land prices are expected to drop some, but so are the prices for grain, hogs, and cattle. Throughout the 20th century, the U.S. government actively aided farmers, but in recent years has attempted to step back from agricultural production. But the state of farming today calls for more government involvement. Some trends that farmers may follow in their efforts to increase income include more diversified crop production; for example, farmers may choose to plant high-oil or high-protein corn, which bring more money in the marketplace. But these new grains also require different methods of storage and marketing. Other farmers are focusing on growing specialty or organic crops or taking advantage of increasing demand for ethanol by planting more corn. (In 2007, U.S. farmers planted nearly 93 million acres of corn—the largest corn crop in 63 years, according to the National Agricultural Statistics Service. As a result of this trend, fewer acres of other crops—such as soybeans and cotton—are being planted.)

Large corporate farms are fast replacing the small farmer, who is being forced out of the industry by the spiraling costs of feed, grain, land, and equipment. The late 1970s and early 1980s were an especially hard time for farmers. Many small farmers were forced to give up farming; some lost farms that had been in their families for generations. Some small-scale farmers, however, have found opportunities in organic food production, farmers' markets, and similar market niches that require more direct personal contact with their customers.

Despite the great difficulty in becoming a farmer today, there are many agriculture-related careers that involve people with farm production, marketing, management, and agribusiness. Those with an interest in farming will likely have to pursue these alternative career paths.

FOR MORE INFORMATION

The AFBF Web site features legislative news, state farm bureau news, online brochures, and information on Farm Bureau programs such as AFBF Young Farmer & Rancher Program. This program, for people ages 18 to 35, offers educational conferences, networking opportunities, and competitive events.
American Farm Bureau Federation (AFBF)
600 Maryland Avenue, SW, Suite 1000W
Washington, DC 20024-2520
Tel: 202-406-3600
http://www.fb.org

For information on certification, contact
American Society of Farm Managers and Rural Appraisers
950 Cherry Street, Suite 508
Denver, CO 80246-2664
Tel: 303-758-3513
http://www.asfmra.org

To learn about farmer-owner cooperatives and how cooperative businesses operate, contact
National Council of Farmer Cooperatives
50 F Street, NW, Suite 900

Washington, DC 20001-1530
Tel: 202-626-8700
http://www.ncfc.org

For information on farm policies, homeland security issues, and other news relating to the agricultural industry, visit the USDA Web site.
U.S. Department of Agriculture (USDA)
1400 Independence Avenue, SW
Washington, DC 20250-0002
Tel: 202-720-2791
http://www.usda.gov

Golf Course Superintendents

OVERVIEW

Golf course superintendents supervise the management and maintenance of the golf course and its associated property, including the golf course and practice areas, golf cart fleet, clubhouse grounds and landscaping, tennis courts, swimming pool, and other recreational facilities, restrooms and potable water on the course, open spaces, wooded areas, and unused acreage. Golf course superintendents supervise the maintenance and repair of machinery and equipment used to maintain the course. They also participate in golf course planning and facility management meetings to advise the management or board of directors on matters regarding the golf course.

HISTORY

Using a bent stick, Roman emperors sent feather-stuffed balls flying through the air in the game, *paganica*. Centuries later in countries throughout Europe, the game had evolved in several variations; the English played *cambuca*, the French played *jeu de mail*, and the Dutch played a version called *het kolven*. The Scottish game *golfe*, however, is the direct ancestor of the modern game. The game became so popular that in 1457, King James II felt he had to ban golfe, along with futeball, in order to guarantee national safety. Apparently, his men were playing the other sports and neglecting their archery skills—skills which were desperately needed to defend Scotland against the English. The ban was finally removed 45 years later.

In 1744, a group of golfe players in Edinburgh formed the first formal golf club, The Company of Gentleman Golfers (now known as the Honourable Company of Edinburgh Golfers). The group established standardized rules which were followed until 10 years later when the Royal and Ancient Golf Club of Saint Andrews was created. This club became the official ruling organization of the sport and, along with the United States Golf Association (USGA), still establishes the rules for the sport. The first golf club and course in the United States was the Saint Andrews Golf Club of Yonkers, established in 1888.

Golf is the only major sport in which the playing field does not conform to specific dimensions or characteristics. In fact, the unique natural features of each golf course are what present the golfer with many of the sport's challenges. A golf course generally has 18 holes spread over a landscaped area, called "greens." Courses usually include a number of hazards aimed at making the game more difficult, such as water, rough, trees, and sand traps (also called bunkers). The distance between each hole varies (from 150 to 600 yards), which also increases the difficulty. Play proceeds from hole to hole until golfers have completed the entire 18 holes. Courses vary in speed, uniformity, texture, graininess, and trueness of the greens. The diverse areas of the golf course require that the individuals caring for it have a wide range of knowledge and expertise in everything from plants to ponds.

Scottish tradition affected more than the game. For a long time, secrets of the art of greenskeeping in the United States were passed from one generation of Scotsmen to the next, and it was even believed that a greenskeeper wasn't skilled unless he was Scottish. Today, the greenskeeper has been replaced by the golf course superintendent, but science hasn't completely replaced art in the caring of golf greens. Observation and experience are as valuable to a golf course superintendent as advanced knowledge in science, business, and communications.

THE JOB

Golf course superintendents supervise the management and maintenance of the golf course and its associated property. They interview, hire, train, direct, and supervise a staff of employees including the following: assistant golf course superintendents, equipment managers, assistant equipment mechanics, horticultural technicians, foremen, office assistants, irrigation specialists, chemical technicians, equipment operators, gardeners, and groundskeepers.

Superintendents plan all maintenance and project work and schedule personnel. They routinely inspect and evaluate projects in progress to be sure the facility's standards are met. In addition to supervising the maintenance and repair of machinery and equipment used on the course, superintendents buy or replace equipment and purchase supplies, such as pesticides and fertilizers. They are responsible for inventory and cost control, keeping operating and capital expenses in line with the established budget.

Course superintendents prepare the annual budgets for the care and maintenance of facility and course properties, attend planning meetings, and are called upon to advise the facility's management or board of directors regarding the golf course. They generally report directly to one of the following individuals: the general manager, the green chairman, the club owner, or the director of parks and recreation. In private club organizations, the superintendent usually must submit plans for course construction, reconstruction, or renovation to the green committee, but he or she does not need to seek approval for the decisions associated with the everyday maintenance of the course and its properties.

REQUIREMENTS

High School

High school courses that will be helpful to you as a prospective golf course superintendent include business, mathematics, earth science, and agriculture. In addition, speech and English classes will help you communicate effectively with employers and coworkers.

Postsecondary Training

Though not required, golf course superintendents typically hold a degree in agronomy, horticulture, or turfgrass management. "For a high school graduate the best path to consider is a four-year bachelor's degree," advises Lanie Griffin, career services manager for the Golf Course Superintendents Association of America (GCSAA). "Students who earn these degrees stand a good chance of securing a job in golf course management. Furthermore, today's trend is the higher the level of education achieved, the broader the opportunities and the better the chances for advancement. Whichever program students choose, it should include courses that will help them develop the business and management skills needed for a successful career in golf course management. These include business administration, finance, communications, a foreign language, personnel management, and public relations courses. Students are encouraged to use electives to establish a strong background in business and communications which will complement agronomic training. Competencies in these areas are essential to a superintendent's professional development."

Agronomy, horticulture, and turfgrass management programs are available at two- and four-year colleges and universities throughout the United States. For a listing, see GCSAA's College Guide at http://www.gcsaa.org.

Certification or Licensing
Many employers prefer to hire course superintendents who are certified by the GCSAA. To be eligible for certification, the candidate must be currently employed as a course superintendent and have a combination of education and experience in the field. Candidates must also submit a portfolio that contains three parts: work samples, skill statements, and case studies. Once a superintendent has been accepted into the GCSAA program, he or she must pass a comprehensive, six-hour examination that covers the game and rules of golf, turfgrass management, pesticides, environmental considerations, financial management, and human resource management. The certification process includes interviews and course evaluations by two certified superintendents. To pass, both certified superintendents must recommend the candidate. Superintendents must renew their certification every five years by documenting continued participation in a wide range of educational activities.

The Sports Turf Managers Association offers the certified sports field manager designation to applicants who complete education and/or experience requirements and who pass an examination that covers the following subjects: agronomics, pest management, administration, and sports specific field management. This certification is available to all who specialize in turf management, including golf course superintendents.

In addition, golf course superintendents need to be familiar with current federal, state, and local laws and regulations related to golf course management, and when necessary, have the proper state certification or licensing as a pesticide applicator.

Other Requirements
"Professionally," says Lanie Griffin, "a superintendent has to be a good communicator and have the ability to manage people; he/she needs the technical and financial skills necessary to oversee the golf course operation. Knowing the agronomic side of golf is important,

but it's equally important to understand the business side of golf. Personally, a superintendent is a hard worker, flexible, and willing to take on challenges, work long hours, and be able to solve problems."

"When we search for golf course superintendents," says Henry DeLozier, vice president of golf for Pulte Homes, a golf course developer, "our top priority is dedication and passion. Next, we look for proven experience. We prefer to hire superintendents who have worked their way up the organization from starter jobs (like weeding and weed-eating) through irrigation repair, to chemical application, to personnel management and leadership. But the most important attribute shared by most successful golf course superintendents is the capacity for leadership. A leader must build support and trust in himself/herself. Then, he or she can show the way and teach employees, members, and customers the features and benefits of a great plan. People must first believe in the leader before they embrace the plan."

EXPLORING

Even before you decide on a school or program in turfgrass management, you should try to get firsthand experience in the field to make certain you are entering a career that you enjoy. During high school, activities geared toward plants and turf management are a good start. Clubs like 4-H and the National FFA Organization (formerly Future Farmers of America) sponsor educational programs, activities, and competitions that revolve around horticulture and agronomy. Even the practical experience of starting and maintaining your own flower or vegetable garden or lawn is something to build on and shows future employers an interest in the field.

A volunteer or part-time job is the next step; begin to build a work history in the field or a related area. Nurseries, public gardens, and parks and recreation offices are involved with the growing and maintenance of flowers and grass. Better yet, apply to the golf course in your area for a position on the groundskeeping crew. No matter how low on the totem pole you may be at first, you have to start somewhere, and, as in most fields, experience counts.

EMPLOYERS

Golf course superintendents are employed by private and public golf courses. Golf is the largest employer of any sport in the United

States, with nearly 16,000 courses employing approximately 235,000 workers.

STARTING OUT

Many schools offer internships or cooperative work programs where students in landscape design or turfgrass management can get school credit for working on a golf course. These programs offer participants the chance to gain valuable on-the-job experience, analyze the business and operation of a golf course, and develop personal contacts and future job placement opportunities. Other schools don't offer these sorts of programs, but leave it up to each student to arrange jobs and internships to acquire experience.

If your school doesn't arrange or provide on-the-job training opportunities, applying for work at golf courses after school hours and during the summer is the best option. In the end, graduates with more hands-on experience will have the greatest chance at jobs. Many new graduates believe they will start at the top of the ranks of golf course superintendents. The truth is, nearly all graduates will probably only find positions as assistant golf course superintendents or crew members. After more work, education, and experience are added to their resumes, they can compete for the position of superintendent.

Participating in a GCSAA student chapter at your college or university is a good way to begin valuable networking in the profession and gain information about golf course internships and available scholarships.

ADVANCEMENT

The field of golf course management is increasingly competitive. Obtaining specialized training or advanced education is one way of advancing to top positions. Others advance through on-the-job experience in supervisory positions.

EARNINGS

According to the GCSAA, the average base salary for golf course superintendents was $73,766 in 2006. Superintendents who supervise 18-hole facilities with budgets over $1 million earned median salaries of $90,000 annually. GCSAA Class A golf course superintendents, especially those who are certified, earn higher salaries. The average salary of GCSAA Class A superintendents was $78,096 in

2006 and certified golf course superintendents averaged $87,225. At least 14 percent of certified golf course superintendents with bachelor's degrees earned $125,000 or more. Assistant golf course superintendents earned an average of $37,032 in 2006.

WORK ENVIRONMENT

On average, the GCSAA reports that most golf course superintendents' time is divided up as follows: golf course maintenance tasks, 36.4 percent; business management tasks, 28.3 percent; personnel management, 28 percent; and other tasks, 7.3 percent. What keeps them indoors are the numerous management tasks, such as balancing the budget and taking inventory. The rest of their time is spent outdoors, on the course itself, in the nursery or other locations on the facilities. Most work year-round, in all kinds of weather, in order to maintain the look of the course. Depending on the geographic location, they may devote more or less time year-round to gardening and grass-cutting duties. For example, the superintendent of a Minnesota course will see his greens under snow for a good portion of the year, while the superintendent of a Florida or Arizona golf course will be managing the greens on his or her course 365 days a year. Which isn't to say that there aren't outdoor tasks during a Minnesota winter; the superintendent is responsible for the health of the trees and plants, as well as the grass. Autumn is spent preparing the grounds and turf for the winter months.

Superintendents work with heavy machinery and chemicals during the maintenance of turf and the application of pesticides. In these instances they must use caution, following safety guidelines to minimize the risk of an injury.

Golf course superintendents work with a wide variety of people, from those actually playing the game to their maintenance staff working on the courses. Patience and diplomacy are required in order to best communicate with guests and staff.

Most golf courses have a greens committee or board of directors. In the case of private country clubs, these boards are usually made up of club members who are nominated to the board for an average period of three years. Board members may have limited understanding of the management of a course; however, they do wield some power as paying club members. As a result, board members' solutions to course management problems may be to fire the superintendent, no matter how unwise a decision that is. Therefore, it is in the best interests of superintendents to develop good negotiating and communication skills. He or she needs to be able to articulate ideas and opinions to the board of directors, and deal firmly with other employees.

OUTLOOK

Although there are nearly 16,000 golf courses in the United States, the number of new golf courses being planned has decreased in recent years, according to the GCSAA. As a result, golf course superintendents will face strong employment competition in coming years. Those with experience, strong educational credentials, and a willingness to continuously upgrade their skills throughout their careers will have the best employment prospects. "It is vital that golf course superintendents stay abreast of the ever evolving changes in the business," says Kevin Carroll, general manager/chief operating officer of The Loxahatchee Club in Jupiter, Florida. "From new technology in equipment and agriculture to improved cultural practices, a superintendent must continue learning and educating him/herself and network with other experts in the industry."

FOR MORE INFORMATION

For comprehensive information on golf course management careers, internships, job listings, approved turfgrass management programs, scholarships, membership, and certification, contact
Golf Course Superintendents Association of America
1421 Research Park Drive
Lawrence, KS 66049-3859
Tel: 800-472-7878
Email: infobox@gcsaa.org
http://www.gcsaa.org

For information on internships, scholarships, and certification, contact
Sports Turf Managers Association
805 New Hampshire, Suite E
Lawrence, KS 66044-2774
Tel: 800-323-3875
http://www.stma.org

For articles and developments in the world of golf, visit the following Web site
Royal and Ancient Golf Club of St. Andrews
http://www.randa.org

INTERVIEW

Anthony Williams is director of grounds for the Stone Mountain Golf Club by Marriott in Stone Mountain, Georgia. He discussed his career with the editors of Careers in Focus: Landscaping and Horticulture.

Q. Please tell us about your career.

A. I am the director of grounds for the Stone Mountain Golf Club by Marriott. I have worked for Marriott Golf for more than 21 years. Marriott Golf is the world's largest resort golf management company, managing 60 courses in 13 countries and serving Marriott, Renaissance, and Ritz Carlton brands. I served my first 20 years with the company at the Renaissance Pinelsle Resort and Golf Club. I worked in support of four Ladies Professional Golf Association World Golf Championships during this time. In 2005, I transferred to my current assignment—the 36-hole (two championship courses) Stone Mountain Golf Club. In my final year at Pinelsle I was honored as the Marriott Golf (all brands) Golf Course Superintendent of the Year.

Q. Why did you decide to become a golf course superintendent?

A. I really wanted to have a career outdoors. I wanted a chance to have a oneness with nature each day and make a good living at the same time. Being a golf course superintendent allows me to do this at a very high level. I am responsible for the management of an amazing green space, and I work with incredibly talented people who are committed to the traditions of the game of golf and the protection of the environment.

Q. Take us through a day in your life on the job.

A. First, we have a department stand-up meeting to hand out job assignments and review goals and projects for the day. The first jobs are all about opening the course for play. Greens, tees, and fairways must be cut and blown. The tee markers and cup locations must be moved, coolers filled, bathrooms cleaned, trash emptied, driving range set up, and a general inspection of the property completed. Then the proshop is given the call to send golfers out with any special instructions (such as please keep the golf carts on the paths—if it has rained—or please use the 90-degree rule when leaving the path). Then we tour the course creating work lists and observing agronomic conditions (asking questions such as will we need to water greens tonight and, if so, how much irrigation will be required). We are also looking for pest activity. We use an integrated pest management philosophy to protect agronomic assets and reduce chemical use, so scouting on a daily basis is critical. For example, if we notice armyworm eggs on a pin flag we know that within a few short weeks they will begin damaging turfgrass. We will need to be prepared to take the appropriate action. After assigning the next duties we check in with the pro shop to make sure the business is running smoothly.

Lunch is usually the next priority unless a tournament or unexpected project (irrigation leak, sudden storm, cart crash, government inspection, financial critique, flat tire, environmental tour, lost tourist, police chase, etc.) comes along. The afternoon ranges from monitoring the moisture levels on our Bentgrass greens, to planting ornamentals, to building birdhouses.

The end of the day is reserved for paperwork. This can include anything from paying the bills, posting work schedules, filling out work logs and chemical logs, returning emails and phone calls, filing, associate reviews, and corporate projects. The day ends with a supervisors meeting to wrap up the day and set up the next day's white board (a huge dry erase board with all assignments and memos of concern).

I can say that each day on the course is exciting. I have seen fawns born, bald eagles in flight, and several avid golfers hit their first (and perhaps their last) hole in one. I have found shed deer antlers, hawk feathers, arrowheads, and countless golf clubs in some interesting places. The average day in a golf course superintendent's life is anything but average.

Q. What advice would you give to high school students who are interested in this career?

A. Always seek excellence when choosing courses, teachers, and friends. I think the National FFA Organization is a great organization for high school students because they teach "life skills" and leadership. This will give you a great cornerstone to build a successful life. I was a very active member in our local FFA, serving as chapter president and attaining my state farmer degree. I also think classes that blend practical skills with theory are the best. For example, if you can teach floral design theory and then give the student the task of making a floral arrangement, then you are passing on valuable knowledge. If it is your dream to be a golf course superintendent then the sooner you can begin blending experience with education the better.

Q. Are you certified? How important is certification to career development and advancement?

A. Yes, I am certified as a golf course superintendent, grounds manager, turfgrass professional, ornamental landscape professional, erosion and sediment control specialist, environmental planner, and pool and spa operator. Certification is very important in the golf industry. I think certification is the best way to validate a successful blend of education and experience. Approximately 9 percent of the members of the Golf Course Superintendents Association of America are certified. These men and women are the trendsetters and leaders of the industry. If you want the advantage of being in the top 10 percent, then you must become certified and maintain certification.

Q. What is one of the most rewarding experiences that you have had in your career?

A. It is hard to pick one as I have been blessed with so many great experiences. However, I recently became the first superintendent in the history of the Golf Course Superintendents Association of America to win back-to-back national Environmental Leaders in Golf Awards (ELGA). I won the National Resort Course ELGA at Renaissance Pinelsle Resort and Golf Club in 2005 and then won the National Public Course and Overall (world champion) ELGA in 2006. This event and the many other events that were made possible by this achievement stand out because it had never been done and was thought to be impossible. I accepted the Overall and National Public Course ELGA at a huge awards presentation in Anaheim, California, in February 2007. That moment on the big stage was pretty special. Since then I have traveled all over the country writing, speaking, and teaching the many positive attributes of an environmentally focused golf operation.

Grounds Managers
and Groundskeepers

QUICK FACTS

School Subjects
Agriculture
Biology

Personal Skills
Following instructions
Mechanical/manipulative

Work Environment
Primarily outdoors
Primarily multiple locations

Minimum Education Level
Bachelor's degree (grounds
  managers)
High school diploma
  (groundskeepers)

Salary Range
$23,940 to $37,300 to
  $60,930 (grounds managers)
$15,120 to $21,260 to
  $34,240 (groundskeepers)

Certification or Licensing
Required for certain
  positions

Outlook
Faster than the average

DOT
408

GOE
03.01.03

NOC
2225

O*NET-SOC
37-1012.00, 37-1012.02,
  37-3011.00, 37-3012.00,
  37-3013.00

OVERVIEW

Grounds managers oversee the maintenance of land and vegetation on sites such as airports, apartment complexes, cemeteries, condominiums, commercial and industrial parks, estates, golf and country clubs, hospitals, military installations, public parks and recreation areas, schools and universities, shopping centers and malls, theme parks, and zoos. They may work alone or supervise a staff of grounds workers. Grounds managers may have their own companies or they may work for one or more landscaping companies. Towns, cities, and large sports facilities often have their own grounds management departments and crews.

Groundskeepers are manual laborers who perform a wide variety of tasks related to a site's maintenance, from hauling tree cuttings to mowing lawns. Approximately 1.5 million grounds maintenance workers are currently employed in the United States.

HISTORY

From ancient Egypt to the present, the exterior landscape surrounding public and private buildings has been as important as the interiors of those structures. Water, plants, trees, and flowers (to name a few elements) add beauty, shade, and form to the landscapes outside of our homes and work environments, among many others. The Hanging Gardens of Babylon (circa 600

80

B.C.), the irrigated gardens at Pasargadae in Persia (sixth century B.C.), and the Romanesque gardens of the Alhambra in Granada (circa A.D. 1377) are all early examples of idyllic settings that, in many ways, have set the standards for landscape designers and grounds managers ever since.

Throughout history, gardens served as places to socialize and exercise, as well as to appreciate nature's beauty. Garden styles changed over the years, from the open loggias and terraced gardens of Renaissance Italy; to the great gardens of Andre Le Notre (1613–1700), who aligned windows with garden paths to create the French Classic Style; to the informal, natural forms of English Landscape Style gardens, where lawns and gardens follow the natural lay of the land, rather than imposed geometries.

Frederick Law Olmstead (1822–1903), an American, was the first to use the term *landscape architecture*. In 1858, Olmstead created the first landscaped area in the United States, New York City's Central Park, based on his impressions of the many different gardening styles he saw on his travels in Europe. Today, the influences of the East and West can be found all over the country, from the Japanese-style roof garden of a Manhattan loft building to the Elizabethan herb garden behind an Iowa farmhouse. No matter where the inspiration originated, each garden owes its beauty to the men and women who spend each day pulling weeds, pruning hedges, and planting new cuttings to maintain the integrity of the design and layout.

THE JOB

Grounds managers are members of a management team who are responsible for the maintenance of a wide variety of public and private sites. Working under the supervision of grounds managers is a crew of groundskeepers, unskilled laborers who work to maintain a site's appearance.

Within the sports industry, grounds managers and their crews work to maintain the condition of playing fields of all different types and the lands surrounding the related facilities. For example, grounds managers and groundskeepers are hired to keep both natural and artificial turf areas in top condition for the sport played on it. In addition to planting the proper type of natural turf or laying artificial turf and ensuring it has excellent drainage, grounds workers regularly mow, fertilize, and aerate the fields. They spray protective pesticides on natural turf to control weeds, kill pests, and prevent diseases or insect infestations from destroying the field's appearance.

Even artificial turf requires special care; grounds managers and their crews must vacuum and disinfect it after a sporting event so that harmful bacteria won't grow and destroy the turf or harm the players who compete on the field. Periodically, the cushioning pad beneath the artificial turf must be replaced. Part of the care for the playing fields includes painting the appropriate boundaries, markers, and team logos and names on the turf, and even retouching them during sporting events.

Grounds managers and groundskeepers also maintain the ornamental grasses, shrubs, plants, and flowers on the grounds of a football stadium, baseball park, or general sports arena.

In addition to the "green" side of the job, grounds managers fulfill specific supervisory duties, such as managing finances, materials, equipment, and staff needed to maintain a playing field and related facilities. For most managers, this means developing goals, scheduling maintenance operations, assigning staff hours, creating budgets, delegating tasks, conducting cost accounting procedures, and hiring, training, and supervising employees.

Golf is the only major sport in which the playing field does not conform to specific dimensions or characteristics. In fact, the varying natural features of each course present the golfer with many of the sport's challenges. As a result, the diverse areas of the golf course require that the individuals caring for it have a wide range of knowledge and expertise in everything from plants to ponds. The groundskeeper working for a golf course performs routine manual labor related to the care of the grass and shrubs, including operating mowers and string trimmers.

Grounds workers implement the designs of landscape architects and designers and then maintain those designs throughout the year. In general, this means they are responsible for planting, pruning, mowing, transplanting, fertilizing, spraying, trimming, training, edging, and any other duties that will keep the landscape looking healthy and attractive. They may work year-round to ensure the quality of the playing fields and other grounds. Depending upon the region of the country, the grounds manager might hire extra groundskeepers during peak periods and cut staff during slower months. In general, spring and summer are the peak seasons, while autumn and winter are much slower. However, schedules depend on the site where grounds managers and groundskeepers work. For example, fall and winter are the busiest times of the year for the grounds workers who maintain the field of a National Football League team.

REQUIREMENTS

High School

Though there are no formal educational requirements for becoming a groundskeeper, grounds managers must have a solid education background to prepare them for a college program. While in high school, study chemistry, biology, and earth science, as well as English, foreign languages, and mathematics. Managers need solid communication skills to work well with their crews and need mathematical ability to balance their budgets and keep other records.

Postsecondary Training

Those interested in becoming grounds managers should aim for a bachelor of science in grounds management, horticulture, agronomy, or a related field. In addition, most employers require that managers have a minimum of four years of experience, at least two in a supervisory position. Grounds managers need to be familiar and comfortable with budgeting, management, and cost-accounting procedures, possess public relations and communication skills, and be current with maintenance issues, such as recycling and hazardous materials. Courses in business management and personnel management are very helpful, although not required.

Most groundskeeping jobs do not require a college degree. Many people working these jobs are either looking to get on-the-job experience or simply trying to make a little extra money. However, some positions involving the application of pesticides, fungicides, and other chemicals do require some educational training.

Certification or Licensing

Grounds professionals who specialize in golf course management can be certified by the Golf Course Superintendents Association of America (GCSAA). To be eligible for certification, the candidate must be currently employed as a course superintendent and have a combination of education and experience in the field. Candidates must also submit a portfolio that contains three parts: work samples, skill statements, and case studies. Once a superintendent has been accepted into the GCSAA's program, he or she must pass a comprehensive, six-hour examination that covers the game and rules of golf, turfgrass management, pesticides, environmental considerations, financial management, and human resource management. The certification process includes interviews and course evaluations by two certified superintendents. To pass, both certified superintendents must recommend the candidate.

The Professional Grounds Management Society offers certification for both grounds managers and workers: the certified grounds manager (CGM) certification and the certified grounds technician (CGT) certification. To be eligible to take the CGM exam, candidates must fulfill one of the following requirements: a bachelor of science degree in a recognized industry field and four years of work in the field of grounds maintenance (including two years of supervisory experience); a two-year degree from a recognized college or junior college and six years of work in the field (including three years of supervisory experience); or eight years in the grounds maintenance field with a minimum of four years of supervisory experience. To take the CGT exam, candidates must have a high school diploma or GED and two years of groundskeeping experience.

The Professional Lawn Care Association of America offers the following designations to applicants who pass examinations: certified landscape professional; certified ornamental landscape professional; certified turfgrass professional; certified turfgrass professional, cool season lawns; certified landscape technician, interior; and certified landscape technician, exterior.

The Sports Turf Managers Association offers the certified sports field manager certification to applicants who meet education and/or experience requirements and pass an examination that covers agronomics, pest management, administration, and sports specific field management.

In the interest of public safety, some states require grounds workers to pass a certification examination on the proper application of pesticides, fungicides, and other harsh chemicals.

Other Requirements

To be a successful grounds manager, you should have good organizational, communication, and leadership skills, and be able to work under deadline pressure. Groundskeepers must be able to follow directions and be responsible, since they are often assigned duties and then asked to work without direct supervision.

EXPLORING

If you are between the ages of five and 22, you might want to join the National Junior Horticulture Association, which offers horticulture-related projects, contests, and other activities. Visit http://www.njha. org for more information.

Groundskeeping positions are excellent entry-level jobs for high school students looking to gain valuable experience. Prior work in a grounds crew can help you later when you are pursuing a career in grounds management. Because most groundskeeping positions are seasonal, you can work part time after school and on weekends during the school year, and full time during the summer. Interested students should start by contacting the municipal parks district, lawn care companies, nurseries, botanical gardens, and professional landscapers in their area to inquire about job possibilities.

EMPLOYERS

There are approximately 1.5 million grounds workers currently employed in the United States. Managers and supervisors hold 184,000 jobs; groundskeepers hold approximately 1.18 million jobs. Grounds workers are employed at golf and country clubs, public parks and recreation areas, apartment complexes, cemeteries, condominiums, estates, schools and universities, shopping centers and malls, theme parks, zoos, commercial and industrial parks, hospitals, airports, and military installations. Cities, towns, and sporting facilities also employ their own grounds management workers. Grounds managers may have their own business or work for one or more landscaping companies.

STARTING OUT

Depending on their experience prior to receiving a degree in agronomy or horticulture, candidates for management positions can start in an entry-level groundskeeping job. Working in a nursery, botanical garden, or park offers the opportunity to learn about the care of plants, flowers, trees, and shrubs. A summer job may evolve into a full-time supervisory position following graduation from a four-year program.

ADVANCEMENT

Advancement usually comes with increased expertise from on-the-job experience (especially in a supervisory position) and additional courses in botany, agronomy, horticulture, and pesticide application. Two- and four-year programs in grounds management, landscape management, turfgrass management, and ornamental horticulture are widely available.

Groundskeepers who acquire additional education and experience can easily advance into management positions. Even a two-year degree can help accelerate a groundskeeper into supervisory jobs.

EARNINGS

Salaries for grounds managers vary depending on level of education, training, and experience. According to the U.S Department of Labor, the median annual salary for supervisors and managers of grounds workers in 2006 was $37,300. The lowest paid 10 percent earned $23,940 annually and the highest paid 10 percent earned more than $60,930.

By comparison, earnings for groundskeepers are much lower. Most groundskeepers only earned between $7.27 and $12.91 an hour (or roughly $15,120 to $26,860 a year) in 2006. Median annual earnings for groundskeepers were $10.22 an hour, or $21,260 a year. The most experienced groundskeepers earned $16.46 or more an hour, or $34,240 or more a year. The low wages are one reason why these jobs are often hard to keep filled, with groundskeeping staff continually leaving to find better-paying work.

The *Chicago Tribune* reports that earnings for groundskeepers employed with a sports team to care for the home stadium are much higher. In 2000, the head groundskeeper for the Chicago White Sox reported earning between $45,000 and $110,000 a year. However, he also reported working up to 110-hour weeks when the Sox were in town!

WORK ENVIRONMENT

For both managerial and nonmanagerial positions, the work is physically demanding, although perhaps more so for groundskeepers. They shovel dirt, haul branches and other cuttings, move large rocks, and dig holes. Grounds managers and groundskeeping crews work outside year-round, in all types and conditions of weather. Management positions, in general, tend to be full time, and as such, are not affected by the seasons. Some portion of a grounds manager's day is spent taking care of administrative duties inside an office. Grounds managers may need to schedule their workers' weekly hours, compute their wages, order chemicals and other supplies, and inventory the tools.

On the other hand, groundskeepers spend nearly all of their day outside, performing primarily manual labor. Groundskeeping jobs, unlike grounds management positions, are seasonal and tied to the heavy demands of spring and summer planting, trimming, and mowing. Landscapers and other employers of groundskeeping crews usually need more staff members during these peak periods and may not promise year-round employment. In more temperate climates, however, such as Florida or Southern California, there is no shortage of year-round jobs.

Grounds managers and groundskeepers for sports facilities are usually under a lot of pressure to complete a job in time for a sports event, and often these sports events are televised, making it that much more important that the football field or baseball diamond looks well cared for.

Pesticides, herbicides, and fungicides are necessary to keep turf, plants, shrubs, trees, and flowers healthy and beautiful. Grounds managers and their crews frequently work with these and other chemicals, and it is essential that they observe safety precautions when applying these chemicals to prevent exposure. Similarly, grounds managers and their crews use many different tools and machines to complete their tasks, from driving a truck or lawn mower, to operating power clippers, chain saws, and sod cutters.

OUTLOOK

The U.S. Department of Labor reports the employment of grounds-keeping professions to grow at a faster rate than the average for all occupations through 2014. Growth is expected in the construction of commercial and industrial buildings, homes, highways, and recreational facilities, which will require grounds maintenance professionals to tend to the general landscaping. Homeowners increasingly rely on landscaping services to maintain the beauty and value of their property. The demand for parks and recreational facilities also can be expected to create demand for grounds maintenance workers. In addition, a high turnover rate, especially among the groundskeeping occupations, offers many opportunities for employment.

Professional sports arenas, stadiums, and fields and the athletes who play in these venues generate billions of dollars. The appearance of a playing field is extremely important to the team and the community that supports it. Fans and sports management alike take great pride in the way their baseball stadium looks, for example, when it is televised in a national broadcast. Grounds managers and their crews will always remain a vital part of maintaining a sports team's image.

FOR MORE INFORMATION

For information on horticultural education, careers, and scholarships, contact

American Society for Horticultural Science
113 South West Street, Suite 200
Alexandria, VA 22314-2851
Tel: 703-836-4606
http://www.ashs.org

For comprehensive information on golf course management careers, internships, job listings, approved turfgrass management programs, and certification, contact
Golf Course Superintendents Association of America
1421 Research Park Drive
Lawrence, KS 66049-3859
Tel: 800-472-7878
Email: infobox@gcsaa.org
http://www.gcsaa.org

For information on student membership and certification, contact
Professional Grounds Management Society
720 Light Street
Baltimore, MD 21230-3816
Tel: 800-609-7467
Email: pgms@assnhqtrs.com
http://www.pgms.org

For information on certification, careers, internships, and student membership, contact
Professional Landcare Network
950 Herndon Parkway, Suite 450
Herndon, VA 20170-5528
Tel: 800-395-2522
http://www.landcarenetwork.org/cms/home.html

For information on internships, scholarships, and certification, contact
Sports Turf Managers Association
805 New Hampshire, Suite E
Lawrence, KS 66044-2774
Tel: 800-323-3875
http://www.stma.org

For profiles of professionals working in a variety of careers, visit
enPlant: Horticulture & Crop Science in Virtual Perspective
http://enplant.osu.edu/index.lasso

For online information on the industry, career leads, and other resources, visit the following Web site:
Landscape Management
http://www.landscapemanagement.net

Horticultural Inspectors

OVERVIEW

Horticultural inspectors are employed by federal, state, and local governments to enforce those laws that protect public health and safety as they pertain to plants and agricultural products.

HISTORY

Federal, state, and local laws have been enacted to provide protection to citizens in many areas of daily life, including horticultural production, storage, and transportation. Over the years, federal, state, and local governments have developed a system of regular inspection and reporting to assure these safety standards are maintained.

Rather than wait until a law has been violated, it is more efficient to employ horticultural inspectors to continuously watch the way in which standards requirements are carried out. Horticultural inspectors enforce compliance with all health and safety laws and regulations that are related to agriculture and horticulture.

THE JOB

Because there are so many areas of horticulture and food production that require regulation, there are different types of specialists within the field of horticultural inspection who determine how compliance with laws can best be met. The following is a list of some of the major kinds of horticultural inspectors employed by the government:

QUICK FACTS

School Subjects
Agriculture
Biology
Health

Personal Skills
Communication/ideas
Technical/scientific

Work Environment
Indoors and outdoors
Primarily multiple locations

Minimum Education Level
Bachelor's degree

Salary Range
$23,930 to $38,100 to $55,620+

Certification or Licensing
Required for certain positions

Outlook
More slowly than the average

DOT
168

GOE
04.04.02

NOC
2263

O*NET-SOC
45-2011.00

Agricultural chemicals inspectors inspect establishments where agricultural service products such as fertilizers, pesticides, and livestock feed and medications are manufactured, marketed, and used. They may monitor distribution warehouses, retail outlets, processing plants, and private and industrial farms to collect samples of their products for analysis. If there is a violation, they gather information and samples for use as legal evidence.

Agricultural-chemical registration specialists review and evaluate information on pesticides, fertilizers, and other products containing dangerous chemicals. If the manufacturers or distributors of the products have complied with government regulations, their applications for registration are approved.

Agricultural commodity graders ensure that retailers and consumers get reliable and safe commodities. They may specialize in cotton, dairy products, eggs and egg products, processed or fresh fruit or vegetables, or grains. The inspectors check product standards and issue official grading certificates. They also verify sanitation standards by means of regular inspection of plants and equipment.

Agriculture specialists work to protect crops, forests, gardens, and livestock from the introduction and spread of plant pests and animal diseases. They act as agricultural experts at ports of entry to help protect people from agroterrorism and bioterrorism, as well as monitor agricultural imports for diseases and harmful pests. They inspect aircraft, ships, railway cars, and other transportation entering the United States for restricted or prohibited plant or animal materials. They also work to prevent the spread of agricultural disease from one state or one part of the country to another.

Disease and insect control field inspectors inspect fields to detect the presence of harmful insects and plant diseases. Inspectors count the numbers of insects on plants or of diseased plants within a sample area. They record the results of their counts on field work sheets. They also collect samples of unidentifiable insects or diseased plants for identification by a supervisor.

Environmental health inspectors, also called *sanitarians,* work primarily for state and local governments to ensure that government standards of cleanliness and purity are met in food, water, and air. They may inspect processing plants, dairies, restaurants, hospitals, and other institutions. Environmental health inspectors in state or local agricultural or health departments may specialize in milk and dairy production, water or air pollution, food or institutional sanitation, or occupational health.

Nursery inspectors work primarily for state and local governments to ensure that nurseries, greenhouses, and garden centers sell disease-free plants, trees, shrubs, and other products. They inspect plants that are imported from other countries, as well as any plants that may be shipped abroad or out of state. Nursery inspectors are knowledgeable about a wide variety of plant pests such as Japanese beetles, gypsy moths, pine shoot beetles, emerald ash borers, and others, as well as plant diseases such as sudden oak death. They also make sure that nurseries have the proper licensing and that workers meet all labor standards established by the U.S. Department of Labor and other federal, state, and local regulating agencies.

REQUIREMENTS

There is such a variety of skills involved in these inspection jobs that the qualifications and education required depend on the area of work.

High School

The minimum education required to be a horticultural inspector is generally a bachelor's degree. High school students should focus on general classes in speech; English, especially writing; business; computer science; and general mathematics. They should also focus on biology, health, chemistry, agriculture, earth science, and shop or vocational training.

Postsecondary Training

The specific degree and training qualifications vary for each position and area in which inspection is done. For federal positions, a civil service examination is generally required. Education and experience in the specific field is usually necessary.

Certification or Licensing

Certification and licensing requirements vary according to the position. Contact the agency for which you would like to work for detailed information on certification and licensing.

Other Requirements

Horticultural inspectors must be precision-minded, have an eye for detail, and be able to accept responsibility. They must be tenacious and patient as they follow each case from investigation to its conclusion. They also must be able to communicate well with others in order to reach a clear analysis of a situation and be able to report this information to a superior or coworker. Inspectors must be able to write effective reports that convey vast amounts of information and investigative work.

EXPLORING

If you are interested in work as a horticultural inspector, you should read magazines about the field. You can also learn more by talking with people who are employed as inspectors and with your high school counselor. Employment in a specific field during summer vacations could be valuable preparation and an opportunity to determine if a general field, such as horticulture, is of interest to you.

EMPLOYERS

The federal government employs the majority of inspectors in certain areas, such as food and agriculture, which fall under the U.S. Public Health Service, the U.S. Department of Agriculture, or the U.S. Department of Homeland Security. Consumer safety is evenly divided between local government and the U.S. Food and Drug Administration.

STARTING OUT

Applicants may enter the occupations by applying to take the appropriate civil service examinations. Education in specific areas may be required. Some positions require a degree or other form of training. Others need considerable on-the-job experience in the field.

The civil service commissions for state and local employment will provide information on health and regulatory inspection positions under their jurisdiction. The federal government provides information on available jobs at local offices of the employment service, at the U.S. Office of Personnel Management (http://www.usajobs.opm.gov). The specific agency concerned with a job area can also be contacted.

ADVANCEMENT

Advancement for horticultural inspectors in the federal government is based on the civil service promotion and salary structure. Advancement is automatic, usually at one-year intervals, for those people whose work is satisfactory. Additional education may also contribute to advancement to supervisory positions.

Advancements for horticultural inspectors in state and local government and in private industry are often similar to those offered at the federal level.

EARNINGS

According to the U.S. Department of Labor, horticultural inspectors earned median wages of $38,100 in 2006. Earnings ranged from less than $23,930 to $55,620 or more annually.

Horticultural inspectors for state and local governments generally earn salaries lower than those paid by the federal government.

Horticultural inspectors also receive other benefits including paid vacation and sick days, health and dental insurance, pensions, and life insurance. Most inspectors enjoy the use of an official automobile and reimbursement for travel expenses.

WORK ENVIRONMENT

Most horticultural inspectors should expect to travel a considerable amount of the time. They will interact with a wide variety of people from different educational and professional backgrounds. Horticultural inspectors sometimes work long and irregular hours. Sometimes, inspectors will experience stressful, unpleasant, and even dangerous situations. Agricultural and food inspectors may be in contact with unpleasant odors, loud noises, potentially infectious diseases, and other difficult working conditions. Agricultural commodity graders may work outside in the heat or in cool refrigeration units. They may also be required to lift heavy objects.

Inspectors may face adversarial situations with individuals or organizations that feel they do not warrant an investigation, are above the law, or are being singled out for inspection.

The work of horticultural inspectors is important and can be rewarding. Compensation and job security are generally good, and travel and automobile expenses are reimbursed when necessary. Inspectors can be proud that the skilled performance of their duties improves life in some way or another for every member of our society.

OUTLOOK

Employment of inspectors is projected to grow more slowly than the average for all occupations through 2014. However, the threat of agroterrorism and bioterrorism and recent national outbreaks of food poisoning have reinforced the need for qualified horticultural inspectors.

FOR MORE INFORMATION

For career information, visit the CBP Web site:
U.S. Customs and Border Protection (CBP)
U.S. Department of Homeland Security
1300 Pennsylvania Avenue, NW
Washington, DC 20229-0001
Tel: 202-344-1130
http://www.customs.ustreas.gov

For information on farm policies, homeland security issues, and other news relating to the agricultural industry, visit the USDA Web site.
U.S. Department of Agriculture (USDA)
1400 Independence Avenue, SW
Washington, DC 20250-0002
Tel: 202-720-2791
http://www.usda.gov

Horticultural Technicians

OVERVIEW

Horticultural technicians cultivate and market plants and flowers that make human surroundings more beautiful. They plant and care for ground cover and trees in parks, on playgrounds, along public highways, and in other areas. They also landscape public and private lands. There are approximately 1.5 million people employed in landscape and horticultural services.

HISTORY

Planting and cultivating gardens is an ancient art form. The famed hanging gardens of Babylon, the formal gardens of Athens, and the terraces and geometric gardens of Italy are early examples of this art. Historically, different countries were renowned for the different types of gardens they cultivated. For instance, Holland distinguished itself by growing dozens of varieties of tulips, and France was known for its fantastic royal gardens. In the 18th century, gardens became more informal and natural, typified by the plantings around George Washington's home, Mount Vernon. In the United States, the first large landscaped area was New York City's Central Park, created in the 1850s. While flowers, parks, and gardens are not as common in the United States as in other countries, a growing enthusiasm is creating a new demand for trained horticultural technicians.

THE JOB

Horticultural technicians usually specialize in one or more of the following areas: floriculture (flowers), nursery operation (shrubs, hedges, and trees), turfgrass (grass), and arboriculture (trees). Most entry-level technicians work as growers, maintenance workers, or salespeople.

The activities of *floriculture technicians* and of *nursery-operation technicians* are closely related. Both kinds of technicians work in nurseries or greenhouses to raise and sell plants. They determine correct soil conditions for specific plants, the proper rooting material for cuttings, and the best fertilizer for promoting growth. They may also be involved with the merchandising aspects of growing plants.

Technicians working in floriculture or nursery operations may become *horticultural-specialty growers* or *plant propagators*. These technicians initiate new kinds of plant growth through specialized techniques both in outdoor fields and under the environmentally controlled conditions of greenhouses and growing sheds. They carefully plan growing schedules, quantities, and utilization schemes to gain the highest quality and most profitable yield. Some of their duties include planting seeds, transplanting seedlings, pruning plants, and inspecting crops for nutrient deficiencies, insects, diseases, and unwanted growth.

In greenhouses and growing sheds, horticultural-specialty growers monitor timing and metering devices that administer nutrients to the plants and flowers. They are also responsible for regulating humidity, ventilation, and carbon dioxide conditions, often using computer programs. They formulate schedules for the dispensing of herbicides, fungicides, and pesticides, and they explain and demonstrate growing techniques and procedures to other workers. Horticultural-specialty growers may also hire personnel, work with vendors and customers, and handle record keeping.

Horticultural technicians working in the area of turfgrass management are involved in the planning and maintenance of commercial lawns and public lands, such as parks, highways, and playing fields. They also work in specialized areas, such as sod production, seed production, irrigation, transportation, and sales of other products and services.

Turfgrass technicians may run their own businesses or work for lawn care services. Private businesses provide lawn care services to homeowners, corporations, colleges, and other large institutions with extensive grounds. These services include mowing, fertilizing, irrigating, and controlling insects, diseases, and weeds. They also

Books to Read

Acquaah, George. *Horticulture: Principles and Practices*. 3d ed. Upper Saddle River, N.J.: Prentice Hall, 2004.

Garner, Jerry. *Careers in Horticulture and Botany*. 2d ed. New York: McGraw-Hill, 2006.

Huxley, Anthony. *The Illustrated History of Gardening*. Guilford, Conn.: The Lyons Press, 1998.

National Gardening Association. *Gardening All-in-One For Dummies*. Hoboken, N.J.: Wiley & Sons, 2003.

Pfahl, John. *Extreme Horticulture*. London, U.K.: Frances Lincoln, 2006.

Reiley, H. Edward. *Introductory Horticulture*. 7th ed. Clifton Park, N.Y.: Thomson Delmar Learning, 2006.

may provide tree and snow removal services and sell lawn care products and equipment. Technicians working in the public sector for local, county, state, or federal government agencies may be involved in designing turfgrass areas in parks or playing fields, or for areas along public highways.

Arboriculture technicians plant, feed, prune, and provide pest control for trees. Self-employed technicians may contract their services to private businesses or a group of companies located in the same industrial park or neighborhood. They care for the trees on the company grounds or in the landscaped areas of industrial parks. Private companies hire arboriculture technicians not only to keep their grounds attractive but also to prevent damage by fallen trees or overgrowth to on-site power lines or other property.

Arboriculture technicians are also employed by local, state, or federal agencies. They decide when and how trees should be removed and where new trees should be placed on public grounds. They work for park and parkway systems, public recreational agencies, and public school systems.

REQUIREMENTS

High School
Many entry-level jobs, especially in landscaping and turfgrass management, are available out of high school. For these positions, the majority of training takes place on the job. To prepare yourself

in high school, take any agricultural classes available, particularly those that include units in botany. Science courses, such as biology, chemistry, and earth science, will also teach you about plant life, development, and the effects of various nutrients. Math, business, and accounting classes will be valuable if you're considering working in retail sales, or running your own business. Also, take English and composition courses to improve your communication skills for preparing reports and assisting in research.

Postsecondary Training

For management and more technical positions, most employers prefer applicants that have an associate's degree in applied science. Many horticulture training programs are available across the country. Programs include horticulture courses in landscape plants, pest management, nursery management, and plant propagation. In addition, students take courses in English composition, small business management, and agribusiness.

Certification or Licensing

Though there are no national certification standards, many states require certification for workers who apply pesticides. Other states require landscape contractors to obtain a license.

Voluntary certification is available to those who want increased opportunities or to advance their career. The Professional Landcare Network offers the following certification designations: certified landscape technician, interior; certified landscape technician, exterior; certified landscape professional; certified turfgrass professional; certified turfgrass professional, cool season lawns; and certified ornamental landscape professional. Other organizations, such as the Professional Grounds Management Society (see the end of this article for contact information), offer additional levels of certification based on education and experience levels.

Other Requirements

To enjoy and succeed in horticulture, you should have an eye for aesthetic beauty and a love of nature. Creative and artistic talents help in arranging flowers in a retail setting or organizing plants in a garden or greenhouse. Horticultural technicians must also possess people skills, as they work closely with professionals as well as clients. If running their own business, technicians need to be detail-oriented, self-motivated, and organized.

EXPLORING

If you've spent a summer mowing lawns for your family or neighbors or kept up a garden in the backyard, then you already have valuable horticulture experience. Many nurseries, flower shops, and local parks or forest preserves use temporary summer employees to work in various capacities. You can also join garden clubs, visit local flower shops, and attend botanical shows to explore the career. The American Public Gardens Association offers internships in public gardens throughout the United States (see the end of this article for contact information).

If you are between the ages of five and 22, you might also want to join the National Junior Horticulture Association, which offers horticulture-related projects, contests, and other activities. Visit http://www.njha.org for more information.

EMPLOYERS

Approximately 1.5 million workers are employed in landscaping, groundskeeping, nursery, greenhouse, and lawn services. The variety of jobs available within the horticultural field provides a number of opportunities. Employers include local parks and recreation departments, botanical gardens, college research facilities, grounds maintenance crews, greenhouses, and lawn care businesses. Sales positions are available for knowledgeable technicians in floral shops, garden stores, and nurseries. Many horticultural technicians are self-employed and run their own lawn care services and greenhouses.

STARTING OUT

Horticulture training programs often offer job placement or internship services. Internships, in turn, may lead to full-time positions with the same employer. Check the classified section of your local newspaper for openings, including those in many chain grocery, hardware, and drugstores with greenhouses and plant departments.

ADVANCEMENT

Nursery-operation and floriculture technicians may advance to a management position in a garden center, greenhouse, flower shop, or other related retail business. These managers are responsible for the entire operation of a retail or wholesale outlet or of a specific department in a business. They maintain inventories, deal with customers and suppliers, hire, train, and supervise employees, direct advertising and promotion activities, and keep records and accounts. Technicians also advance to work as *horticultural inspectors,* who work for local, state, or federal governments. Arboriculture technicians find opportunities as garden superintendents, tree surgeons, and park supervisors. Turfgrass technicians may advance to such positions as grounds superintendent, commercial sod grower, consultant, or park/golf course supervisor.

With additional experience and education (usually a degree from a four-year institution), some floriculture and nursery-operation technicians become *horticulturists,* either at a research facility or a large firm. Horticulturists conduct experiments and investigations into problems of breeding, production, storage, processing, and transit of fruits, nuts, berries, vegetables, flowers, bushes, and trees. They develop new plant varieties and determine methods of planting, spraying, cultivating, and harvesting.

Many advancement opportunities in this field require technicians to start their own businesses. This requires sufficient funds and the willingness to commit one's own financial resources to career development.

EARNINGS

Because of the wide range of jobs available to horticultural technicians, average hourly salaries vary from minimum wage to more than $20 an hour (which translates into approximately $12,168 to $41,600 or more per year). According to U.S. Department of Labor data, in 2006 landscaping and groundskeeping workers earned an average of $10.22 an hour (approximately $21,260 annually for full-time work). With more experience, managers of landscaping, lawn service, and groundskeeping workers earned an average of $16.46 an hour (approximately $34,240 annually). Fringe benefits vary from employer to employer, but generally include hospitalization and other insurance coverage, retirement benefits, and educational assistance. Self-employed workers, however, have to arrange for their own benefits.

WORK ENVIRONMENT

Horticultural technicians generally work a 40-hour week. Those who work in parks are often required to work weekends and some summer evenings. Whether working indoors in a greenhouse or florist shop, or outdoors in a park or on a golf course, they are surrounded by beauty. However, the job comes in all kinds of weather. Arboriculture technicians, landscape developers, and turfgrass technicians spend a good deal of time outdoors and occasionally must work in rain, mud, or extreme temperatures.

Some technicians, such as those who work in greenhouses, public gardens, and floral shops, work in fairly peaceful surroundings and are able to enjoy the products of their work—the flowers or plants they tend. Jobs can also be exhausting and strenuous. Depending on the job, workers may have to climb trees, lift large equipment, mow large lawns, or kneel and bend to care for plants and soil. Some of the machinery used, such as blower vacs and mowers, can be very noisy. In addition, depending on the nature of the work, technicians may have to handle chemicals.

OUTLOOK

According to the U.S. Department of Labor, employment for horticultural technicians is expected to grow faster than the average for all occupations through 2014. High turnover in the business continually provides openings. Many horticultural technicians work only part time, so employers are often looking to fill vacant positions. Because wages for beginning workers are low, employers have difficulty attracting enough workers.

The continued development and redevelopment of urban areas, such as the construction of commercial and industrial buildings, shopping malls, homes, highways, and parks, contribute to the steady growth of employment opportunities for horticulture technicians. An increased interest in lawn care and the environment also has created a demand for skilled workers. There is a wider public awareness of the benefits of lawn care, such as safer yards for children to play in, more attractive surroundings for family relaxation and entertaining, and increased home value. To care for their property while conserving leisure time, homeowners are expected to continue to use professional lawn care services.

On the other hand, many homeowners like to care for their landscaping themselves. To cater to this consumer, many retail chain stores, from drugstores to hardware stores, greatly expand their lawn and garden centers every spring and summer and need knowledgeable horticultural workers on staff.

FOR MORE INFORMATION

To learn more about special gardening programs, and to get other information about public gardens, contact

American Public Gardens Association
100 West 10th Street, Suite 614
Wilmington, DE 19801-6604
Tel: 302-655-7100
http://www.publicgardens.org

For information on student membership and certification, contact

Professional Grounds Management Society
720 Light Street
Baltimore, MD 21230-3816
Tel: 800-609-7467
Email: pgms@assnhqtrs.com
http://www.pgms.org

For information on certification, careers, internships, and student membership, contact

Professional Landcare Network
950 Herndon Parkway, Suite 450
Herndon, VA 20170-5528
Tel: 800-395-2522
http://www.landcarenetwork.org

Horticultural Therapists

OVERVIEW

Horticultural therapists combine their love of plants and nature with their desire to help people improve their lives. They use gardening, plant care, and other nature activities as therapy tools for helping their clients to feel better by doing such things as focusing on a project, improving social skills, and being physically active. In addition to these benefits, clients experience emotional benefits, such as feeling secure, responsible, and needed. Horticultural therapists' clients can include nursing home residents, psychiatric patients, prison inmates, "at risk" youth, and the mentally disabled. Frequently horticultural therapists work as part of a health care team, which may include doctors, physical therapists, nurses, social workers, and others.

HISTORY

Gardens have been grown for thousands of years, both for their beauty as well as their products. In the Middle Ages, for example, gardening took place mainly within the walls of monasteries, and gardens included herbs for medicinal purposes, flowers for the church, and fruits and vegetables for the monks to eat. In the United States, people also gardened for pleasure as well as practicality. With the opening of the Friends Asylum for the Insane in Pennsylvania in 1817, however, gardening and nature activities took on an additional purpose. The Friends Asylum, a hospital for the mentally ill, was built on a farm and had walkways, gardens, and tree-filled areas. As part of their treatment, patients were expected to participate in the upkeep of the grounds. In 1879, the Friends Asylum built a greenhouse for patient use and today is recognized as the first-known U.S. hospital to treat patients with what is now known as horticultural therapy.

The use of horticultural therapy did not become popular, however, until after World War II. Garden club groups, wanting to help wounded servicemen at veterans' hospitals, began volunteering and sharing their gardening know-how. By 1955, Michigan State University was the first university to award an undergraduate degree in horticultural therapy. Today horticultural therapists undergo special training, and a number of colleges and universities offer degrees or programs in horticultural therapy.

THE JOB

During an average workday, horticultural therapists usually spend much of their time working directly with clients. In addition to working with clients, horticultural therapists who hold management positions need to spend time managing staff, arranging schedules, and perhaps overseeing the work of volunteers. One of horticultural therapists' most important responsibilities is to assign the right task to each client so that their skills are enhanced and their confidence is boosted. After all, clients who are already depressed, for example, won't feel much better when the hard-to-grow plants that they were assigned to watch over suddenly die. In order to determine what projects will suit their clients, horticultural therapists begin by assessing each client's mental and physical state. This assessment may involve talking to the clients, reviewing medical records, and consulting with a physician or other health care professional about a treatment plan.

With the results from the assessment, therapists determine what kind of work will benefit the client. Therapists then assign the client a job. Therapists and clients may work in greenhouses, in outdoor garden areas on hospital grounds, in classroom-type settings to which the therapists have brought all the necessary supplies, or at community botanical gardens, to name a few locations. Depending on the work area, a client may be asked to put soil in cups to plant seeds, water a garden, or be part of a group activity in which something will be made from the garden's products, such as tea or dried flower arrangements. In some cases, the gardens' produce and plants are sold to help pay for expenses, such as the purchasing of new seeds and plants. In this way, clients may be involved in business goals and continue to develop their sense of accomplishment.

Establishing a place where clients can feel safe and useful is an important part of horticultural therapists' work. This may mean allowing clients to work at their own pace to complete a task, giving praise for accomplishments (no matter how small), encouraging clients to talk to each other to decrease feelings of loneliness, and ensuring that the atmosphere of the therapy session stays positive. Horticultural therapist Lorraine Hanson explains, "One of the benefits of this treatment is that patients get a chance to socialize with each other while they work. They look forward to that, and it helps them prepare to reenter their communities."

In addition to working with clients, horticultural therapists who are part of a health care team will likely need to spend some of their time attending meetings with other team members to report on a client's progress and discuss a continuing treatment plan. Horticultural therapists must also do some paperwork, keeping their own records about clients, projects that have been completed, and even expenses. A successful horticultural therapist must have creativity in order to think of new projects for clients to work on as well as figuring out how to tailor projects and tasks to meet the needs of each client.

Because horticultural therapists often work with clients who have profound or complex problems, such as people with Alzheimer's disease, they may be faced with situations in which the client doesn't improve or doesn't feel the therapy has been helpful. This can be frustrating and even discouraging for the therapist, but it is also an aspect of the job that each therapist needs to deal with.

Some horticultural therapists also provide consulting services, usually to architects, designers, and administrators of health care or human services facilities. For example, they may offer their professional advice during the building or redesigning of hospitals, schools, and assisted-living communities. They may help with landscaping, selecting plants that are suitable for the region and offer a variety of colors, shapes, and smells. They may advise on the creation of "barrier free" gardens that are accessible to those with disabilities. And, they may work on the design of interior spaces, such as greenhouses and solariums.

REQUIREMENTS

High School
You can begin to prepare for this career while you are still in high school. Science classes are important to take, including biology,

chemistry, and earth science, which should all give you a basic understanding of growth processes. If your school offers agriculture classes, particularly those dealing with plants, be sure to take them. To learn about different groups of people and how to relate to them, take sociology and psychology classes. English classes will help you develop your communication skills, which are vital in this profession. Other important classes to take to prepare you for college and work include mathematics, economics, and computer science.

Postsecondary Training
Horticultural therapy has only fairly recently been recognized as a profession in this country (as you recall, the first undergraduate degree in the field was given in 1955), and routes to enter this field have not yet become firmly established. To become registered by the American Horticultural Therapy Association (AHTA), however, you will need at least some related educational experience. Those in the field recommend that anyone wanting to work as a horticultural therapist should have, at a minimum, a bachelor's degree. A number of colleges offer degrees in horticultural therapy or horticulture degrees with a concentration in horticultural therapy, including Kansas State University, Rutgers University, and the University of Maine–Orono. The AHTA provides a listing of schools offering these programs on its Web site, http://www.ahta.org. Course work generally includes studies in botany, plant pathology, soil science, psychology, group dynamics, counseling, communications, business management, and economics, to name a few areas. In addition, an internship involving direct work with clients is usually required. Other facilities, such as botanic gardens, may offer certificate programs, but, naturally, these programs are much smaller in scope than horticulture degree programs.

Certification or Licensing
The AHTA offers voluntary certification in the form of the horticultural therapist registered (HTR) designation. Applicants for the HTR credential must have a four-year college degree (with required course content in horticulture, human services, and horticultural therapy) and complete a 480-hour internship (field work) under the supervision of an AHTA-registered horticultural therapist. Currently no licensing exists for horticultural therapists.

Other Requirements
Horticultural therapists must have a strong desire to help people, enjoy working with diverse populations, and be able to see each

client as an individual. Just as important, of course, horticultural therapists must have an interest in science, a love of nature, and a "green thumb." These therapists need to be creative, perceptive, and able to manage groups. They must be able to interact with a variety of professionals, such as doctors, social workers, administrators, and architects, and work well as part of a team. As therapists, they may develop close emotional relationships with their clients, but they also must stop themselves from becoming emotionally over involved and realize the limits of their responsibilities. This work can often be quite physical, involving lifting and carrying, outdoor work, and work with the hands, so horticultural therapists should be in good physical shape.

EXPLORING

There are a number of ways you can explore your interest in this field. No matter where you live, become involved in gardening. This may mean gardening in your own backyard, creating a window box garden, or working at a community garden. To increase your gardening knowledge, join gardening groups and read about gardening on Web sites such as those by the National Gardening Association and the Garden Club of America (see the end of this article for contact information). Such sites usually provide tips for gardeners as well as information on gardening events. Volunteer at a local public facility, such as a museum with a garden, a botanic garden, or a nature trail, to meet others interested in and knowledgeable about gardening. Keep up-to-date by reading gardening magazines and talking to professionals, such as greenhouse managers. You can also get a part-time or summer job at a gardening supply store, greenhouse, or even the floral section of a grocery store.

Of course, it is just as important to explore your interest in working with people who need some type of assistance. Therefore, get paid part-time or summer work at a nursing home, hospital, assisted-care facility, or even a daycare center. If you are unable to find paid work, get experience by volunteering at one of these places.

EMPLOYERS

Hospitals, rehabilitation centers, botanical centers, government social service agencies, and prisons are among the institutions that may employ horticultural therapists. In addition, horticultural therapists may work independently as consultants.

STARTING OUT

An internship completed during your college years provides an excellent way to make contacts with professionals in the field. These contacts may be able to help you find a job once you graduate. Also, by joining the AHTA, you will be able to network with other professionals and find out about job openings. Your school's career center may be able to provide you with information about employers looking to hire horticultural therapists. You can also apply directly to facilities such as hospitals, nursing homes, and botanical centers.

ADVANCEMENT

Advancement in this profession typically comes with increased education and experience. Horticultural therapists may advance by becoming registered at the horticultural therapist master (HTM) level, moving into management positions, and overseeing the work of other therapists on staff. Some may advance by adding consulting to their current responsibilities. Others may consider it an advancement to move into consulting full time. Still others may move into teaching at schools offering horticultural therapy programs.

EARNINGS

The U.S. Department of Labor reports that the median annual earnings of recreational therapists were $34,990 in 2006. Salaries ranged from less than $20,880 to more than $55,530 a year. Rehabilitation counselors had median annual earnings of $29,200 and mental health counselors had median earnings of $34,380.

According to the most recent AHTA survey available, beginning horticulture therapists make approximately $25,315. Those with five to 10 years of experience have annual earnings of approximately $31,750, and those with more than 10 years of experience earn approximately $36,295.

Benefits will depend on the employer but generally include standard ones, such as paid vacation and sick days and health insurance. Those who work as independent consultants will need to provide for their own health insurance and other benefits.

WORK ENVIRONMENT

Horticultural therapists work in many different environments. Big city community gardens, classrooms, greenhouses, and hospital psychiatric wards are just a few of the settings. Work environments, therefore, can include being outdoors in the sun all day; being in a locked facility, such as for psychiatric patients or prisoners; being in a warm, stuffy greenhouse; and being in an air-conditioned school. No matter where horticultural therapists work, though, they are in the business of helping people, and they spend most of their day interacting with others, such as clients, doctors, and volunteers. Because the therapists try to create calm, safe environments for their clients, the environments the therapists spend much of their time working in will be calm as well. Horticultural therapists shouldn't mind getting a bit dirty during the course of the day; after all, they may need to demonstrate activities such as planting a row of seeds in wet soil.

OUTLOOK

The outlook for horticultural therapists is good. The U.S. Department of Labor reports that counselors will have faster-than-average employment growth, while recreational therapists will have slower-than-average employment growth. As horticultural therapy gains recognition both from professionals and the public, the demand for it is likely to increase.

One factor that may affect the availability of full-time jobs in hospitals is the cost-cutting measures used by managed care and other insurance companies to severely limit patients' hospital stays. However, this may create more opportunities for those working at outpatient centers and other facilities.

FOR MORE INFORMATION

For more information on the career, schools with horticultural therapy programs, registration, and publications, contact
American Horticultural Therapy Association
201 East Main Street, Suite 1405
Lexington, KY 40507-2004
Tel: 800-634-1603
Email: info@ahta.org
http://www.ahta.org

To learn more about gardening, contact the following associations:
American Community Gardening Association
1777 East Broad Street
Columbus, OH 43203-2040

Tel: 877-275-2242
Email: info@communitygarden.org
http://www.communitygarden.org

Garden Club of America
14 East 60th Street, 3rd Floor
New York, NY 10022-7147
Tel: 212-753-8287
http://www.gcamerica.org

National Gardening Association
1100 Dorset Street
South Burlington, VT 05403-8000
Tel: 802-863-5251
http://www.garden.org

Horticulturists

OVERVIEW

Horticulturists are agricultural scientists who conduct experiments and investigations into problems of breeding, production, storage, processing, and transit of fruits, nuts, berries, vegetables, flowers, bushes, and trees. They develop new plant varieties and determine more effective methods of planting, spraying, cultivating, and harvesting. Besides agricultural research, horticulturists may be employed in retail or recreation sectors. The field of horticulture can be divided into four main specialties—*arboriculture*, the study and cultivation of trees; *floriculture*, the study and cultivation of flowering and ornamental plants; *olericulture*, the study and cultivation of vegetables; and *pomology*, the study and cultivation of fruits and nuts.

HISTORY

The beginnings of horticulture can be traced back to when humankind evolved from a primitive and nomadic existence to one more rooted to a particular area. Plants were not only used for nourishment, but medicinal purposes as well. Early civilizations came to recognize the benefits of certain herbs, plants, and flowers, and passed this knowledge from generation to generation. Through subsequent generations they experimented informally and formally (as horticulturists, plant breeders, and other plant scientists) in an attempt to improve the quality and productivity of these food and medicinal resources.

Many horticulturists belong to the American Society of Horticultural Science (ASHS), a century old group dedicated to the advancement, education, and application of horticultural research.

THE JOB

Horticulturists conduct research and experiments to create new or improved breeds of plants, fruits, and vegetables that are better tasting, or able to withstand extremes of weather or soil condition and disease or pests. Other plants are altered to fit a specific need, such as easier harvesting, packaging, or shipping.

Horticulturists use computers and related technology to conduct much of their research. For example, horticultural scientists employed by the U.S. Department of Agriculture may help create crop simulation models, computer programs that are used to predict the growth and development of crops. Scientists input data regarding the soil type of a specific area, weather conditions, and other information to predict the yield, maturity date, and other elements of crop production. Farmers, especially those in developing areas, use this information to make educated choices about the types of crops to cultivate. Horticulturists have also developed computer

A horticulturist (left) and plant pathologist inspect greenhouse plants for pecan scab damage. *(Rob Flynn, Agricultural Research Service, U.S. Department of Agriculture)*

technology to gauge the ripeness of fruit, creating a faster and less-invasive way to test and sort thousands of apples, peaches, melons, and other fruit before they go to market. They use finely calibrated sensors to measure the frequency of sound waves against a piece of fruit. Random pieces of fruit such as apples are tested to check for a certain level of sound waves—once reached, the apple crop is considered ready for harvest.

Many horticulturists are employed by large food-production companies. For example, the Heinz Company may have a team of horticulturists specializing in pomology assigned to its tomato-breeding program. Horticulturists in this program may breed new hybrids of hardy, high-yielding tomato plants. They plant and care for seedlings in greenhouses or other temperature-controlled settings, or perhaps on a company farm. Data—such as the size of each plant and fruit, growth rate, and taste—are carefully documented for as long as five growing seasons. Any complications or diseases, such as bacterial wilt and early blight, which occurred during growth are also recorded. This program may create hundreds of different hybrids annually, but only a very few are considered exceptional enough to market to tomato processors and farmers.

Horticulturists also conduct research for the landscaping industry. For example, researchers might study different species of native and ornamental grasses. Grass plugs might be planted in various grades of soil and exposed to different propagation times and varying levels of fertilizer or compost. The ability of grasses to seed is also monitored. Horticulturists will record several years of research data before making a recommendation on the grass best suited for a particular landscaping setting.

REQUIREMENTS

High School
High school students can prepare for a career as a horticulturist by taking a course load heavy in mathematics and science (including classes in agricultural science, horticultural science, biology, earth science, environmental science, and chemistry). English and speech classes will help you to write reports and communicate effectively with coworkers.

Postsecondary Training
You will need at least a bachelor's degree in horticulture to work in this field. Many colleges and universities throughout the United States offer degrees in horticulture. Visit http://www.ashs.org/

colleges for a list of colleges and universities that offer programs in horticulture.

In 1923, Cornell University founded the first chapter of Pi Alpha Xi—an honor society specifically for horticulture students. Currently, Pi Alpha Xi has 13,000 members at 39 chapters at colleges and universities throughout the United States. Visit http://www.pax.okstate.edu/paxchapt.html for more information.

Certification or Licensing

Certification, while not a necessity, is helpful to horticultural professionals who want to pursue a higher level of knowledge within their field. Two horticulture organizations offer certification programs. The American Society of Agronomy offers the certified professional agronomist and certified crop adviser designations. The American Society for Horticultural Science offers the certified professional horticulturist designation. Contact these organizations for more information on certification requirements.

Other Requirements

To be a successful horticulturist, you should have a deep love of science and a strong curiosity about the nature of plants and their environments. You should also be self-motivated in order to perform research, be able to work well with others, be an effective communicator, and have physical stamina in order to conduct field research in sometimes demanding weather conditions.

EXPLORING

You can explore the basic duties of a horticulturist by growing vegetables and other plants in your backyard or in another setting. Track the progress of each plant by recording when it was planted, the amount of sunlight it receives, the type of soil used for planting, type of fertilizer used, and other factors that affect growth. Analyze why each plant was successful or not and apply your research the next time you plant to create healthier and heartier plants.

Another way to learn about this field is to get involved in horticulture-related extracurricular activities or organizations at your high school. Ask your science teacher to arrange an information interview with a horticulturist.

You may also want to join groups such as the National FFA Organization (http://www.ffa.org) to learn more about a career in horticulture. If you are between the ages of five and 22, you can join the National Junior Horticulture Association, which offers horticulture-related projects, contests, and other activities. Visit http://www.njha.org for more information.

EMPLOYERS

Job opportunities in horticulture can be found with a variety of employers. Government agencies such as the Agricultural Research Service of the U.S. Department of Agriculture often hire horticulture graduates to conduct research and experiments to help improve the quality of crops. In fact, the federal government employs 25 percent of all agricultural scientists. Research jobs can also be found with private companies such as Bayer Crop Science, Kraft Foods, or ConAgra Foods.

Profile: Luther Burbank (1849–1926)

Luther Burbank was a U.S. horticulturist who introduced more than 800 new plant varieties, including more than 200 varieties of fruits, vegetables, flowers, and grasses, including the thornless Opuntia cactus, the plumcot (a fruit that is a cross between the plum and the apricot), and the Burbank potato (which is larger and hardier than potatoes grown at the time).

Burbank was born in Lancaster, Massachusetts. He spent his early years on a farm, and at age 21, purchased land near Lunenburg, Massachusetts, and began to experiment with plant breeding.

In 1872, Burbank developed his most famous hybrid, the Burbank potato. He used funds from the sale of the rights to this product to purchase a greenhouse and nursery in Santa Rosa, California. For the next 50-plus years, Burbank conducted countless experiments and developed new varieties of apples, peaches, nuts, and flowers (such as the Shasta daisy, which is a combination of the wild American daisy, the Japanese daisy, and the English daisy).

When Burbank died in 1926, he was working on more than 3,000 experiments.

Burbank's writings include *The Training of the Human Plant* (1907), *Luther Burbank: His Methods and Discoveries* (12 volumes, 1914–15), and *How Plants Are Trained to Work for Man* (8 volumes, 1921).

Source: *New Standard Encyclopedia*

STARTING OUT

Many horticulturists begin their careers with entry-level positions as research assistants. A college degree, combined with field experience, will allow the individual to earn promotions to more skilled and higher paying jobs.

Some horticultural students opt for internships as a way to gain industry experience, as well as establish contacts. If their internships go well, students may be offered full-time positions after graduation. The ASHS offers internship placement assistance during its annual conference, allowing a venue for students and potential employers to meet.

ADVANCEMENT

Solid work experience can lead to advancement to jobs with more responsibility and higher pay. Some horticulture students choose to continue their studies in order to make them more desirable for management positions. A master's degree or Ph.D. in horticulture is helpful for students pursuing a career in research or academics.

EARNINGS

Soil and plant scientists (including horticulturists) earned median annual salaries of approximately $56,080 in 2006, according to the U.S. Department of Labor. Salaries ranged from less than $33,650 to $93,460 or more per year. Soil and plant scientists employed by the federal government had mean annual earnings of $67,530.

Horticulturists typically receive health and retirement benefits in addition to their annual salary.

WORK CONDITIONS

Employment conditions can vary greatly depending on the specialty of the horticulturist. Those conducting agricultural research, for example, may spend a large part of the year working indoors in an office setting. They often use temperature-controlled plant chambers to germinate seeds, or cultivate new varieties of seedlings. Researchers also conduct their experiments in greenhouses and outdoors in test gardens and fields. They may work with area farmers to determine more cost effective methods of harvesting and processing their crops.

Individuals who are sensitive to extreme weather conditions or highly allergic to pollen or certain plants should carefully consider entry into this career. Potential exposure to agricultural chemicals, some quite hazardous, is also a downside of being a horticulturist.

OUTLOOK

Employment for horticulturists is expected to grow about as fast as the average for all occupations through 2014, according to the U.S. Department of Labor. Horticulturists will continue to be needed to help produce crops that create better yields, that are more resistant to plant pathogens and pests, and that can adapt to areas in which soil and water quality, as well as water shortages, are major issues. Horticulturists with master's degrees—especially those interested in working in applied research positions in a laboratory—will have the best employment prospects.

FOR MORE INFORMATION

For information on careers and horticultural research, contact the following agencies of the U.S. Department of Agriculture:
Agricultural Research Service
U.S. Department of Agriculture
1400 Independence Avenue, SW
Washington, DC 20250-0002
Tel: 202-720-3656
http://www.ars.usda.gov

U.S. Horticultural Research Laboratory
U.S. Department of Agriculture
Agricultural Research Service
2001 South Rock Road
Fort Pierce, FL 34945-3030
Tel: 772-462-5800
http://www.ars.usda.gov/Main/docs.htm?docid=7376

For information on internships, certification, membership, and career opportunities, contact
American Society for Horticultural Science
113 South West Street, Suite 200
Alexandria, VA 22314-2851
Tel: 703-836-4606
http://www.ashs.org

For information on careers and certification, contact
American Society of Agronomy
677 South Segoe Road
Madison, WI 53711-1086
Tel: 608-273-8080
http://www.agronomy.org

For more information on agricultural careers and student programs, contact
National FFA Organization
6060 FFA Drive
PO Box 68960
Indianapolis, IN 46268-0960
Tel: 317-802-6060
http://www.ffa.org

This association helps young people learn more about the field of horticulture through projects, contests, and other activities. Its Web site offers informative videos about various careers in the industry.
National Junior Horticulture Association
15 Railroad Avenue
Homer City, PA 15748-1378
Tel: 724-479-3254
http://www.njha.org

Landscape Architects

OVERVIEW

Landscape architects plan and design areas such as highways, housing communities, college campuses, commercial centers, recreation facilities, and nature conservation areas. They work to balance beauty and function in developed outdoor areas. There are approximately 25,000 landscape architects employed in the United States.

HISTORY

In the United States, landscape architecture has been practiced as a profession for the last 100 years. During the early part of the 20th century, landscape architects were employed mainly by the wealthy or by the government on public-works projects. In 1918, the practice of dividing large plots of land into individual lots for sale was born. In addition, there was a new public interest in the development of outdoor recreational facilities. These two factors provided many new opportunities for landscape architects.

The most dramatic growth occurred following the environmental movement of the 1960s, when public respect for protection of valuable natural resources reached an all-time high. Landscape architects have played a key role in encouraging the protection of natural resources while providing for the increasing housing and recreation needs of the American public.

In the last 30 years, the development of recreational areas has become more important as has the development of streets, bypasses, and massive highways. Landscape architects are needed in most projects of this nature. Both developers and community planners draw upon the services of landscape architects now more than ever.

THE JOB

Landscape architects plan and design outdoor spaces that make the best use of the land and at the same time respect the needs of the natural environment. They may be involved in a number of different types of projects, including the design of parks or gardens, scenic roads, housing projects, college or high school campuses, country clubs, cemeteries, or golf courses. Both the public and private sectors employ them.

Landscape architects begin a project by carefully reviewing their client's desires, including the purpose, structures needed, and funds available. They study the work site itself, observing and mapping such features as the slope of the land, existing structures, plants, and trees. They also consider different views of the location, taking note of shady and sunny areas, the structure of the soil, and existing utilities.

Landscape architects consult with a number of different people, such as engineers, architects, city officials, zoning experts, real estate agents and brokers, and landscape nursery workers to develop a complete understanding of the job. Then they develop detailed plans and drawings of the site to present to the client for approval. Some projects take many months before the proposed plans are ready to be presented to the client.

After developing final plans and drawing up a materials list, landscape architects invite construction companies to submit bids for the job. Depending upon the nature of the project and the contractual agreement, landscape architects may remain on the job to supervise construction, or they may leave the project once work has begun. Those who remain on the job serve as the client's representative until the job is completed and approved.

REQUIREMENTS

High School

To prepare for a college program in landscape architecture, you should take courses in English composition and literature; social sciences, including history, government, and sociology; natural sciences, including biology, chemistry, and physics; and mathematics. If available, take drafting and mechanical drawing courses to begin building the technical skills needed for the career.

Postsecondary Training

A bachelor's or master's degree in landscape architecture is usually the minimum requirement for entry into this field. Undergraduate and graduate programs in landscape architecture are offered in various colleges and universities; 79 programs at 62 colleges and universities are accredited by the Landscape Architectural Accreditation Board of the American Society of Landscape Architects (ASLA). Courses of study usually focus on six basic areas of the profession: landscape design, landscape construction, plants, architecture, graphic expression (mechanical, freehand, and computer-based drawings), and verbal expression.

Hands-on work is a crucial element to the curriculum. Whenever possible, students work on real projects to gain experience with computer-aided design programs and video simulation.

Certification or Licensing

Almost all states require landscape architects to be licensed. To obtain licensure, applicants must pass the Landscape Architect Registration Examination, sponsored by the Council of Landscape Architectural Registration Boards (CLARB). Though standards vary by state, most require applicants to have a degree from an accredited program and to be working toward one to four years of experience in the field. In addition, 14 states require prospective landscape architects to pass another exam that tests knowledge of local environmental regulations, vegetation, and other characteristics unique to the particular state. Because these standards vary, landscape architects may have to reapply for licensure if they plan to work in a different state. However, in many cases, workers who meet the national standards and have passed the exam may be granted the right to work elsewhere. For more information on licensing, contact the CLARB (http://www.clarb.org) or the ASLA (http://www.asla.org).

Landscape architects working for the federal government need a bachelor's or master's degree but do not need to be licensed.

Other Requirements

You should be interested in art and nature and have good business sense, especially if you hope to work independently. Interest in environmental protection, community improvement, and landscape design is also crucial for the profession. You should also be flexible and be able to think creatively to solve unexpected problems that may develop during the course of a project.

EXPLORING

If you are interested in learning more about the field, you can gather information and experience in a number of ways. Apply for a summer internship with a landscape architectural firm or at least arrange to talk with someone in the job. Ask them questions about their daily duties, the job's advantages and disadvantages, and if they recommend any landscape architecture programs. Finally, you can take the Landscape Architecture Interest Test at the Web site (http://www. asla.org/nonmembers/recruitment/lainttest.htm) of the American Society of Landscape Architects to gauge your interest in the field.

EMPLOYERS

There are approximately 25,000 landscape architects employed in the United States. Landscape architects work in every state in the United States, in small towns and cities as well as heavily populated areas. Some work in rural areas, such as those who plan and design parks and recreational areas. However the majority of positions are found in suburban and urban areas.

Landscape architects work for a variety of different employers in both the public and private sectors. They may work with a school board planning a new elementary or high school, with manufacturers developing a new factory, with homeowners improving the land surrounding their home, or with a city council planning a new suburban development.

In the private sector, most landscape architects do some residential work, though few limit themselves entirely to projects with individual homeowners. Larger commercial or community projects are usually more profitable. Workers in the public sector plan and design government buildings, parks, and public lands. They also may conduct studies on environmental issues and restore lands such as mines or landfills.

STARTING OUT

After graduating from a landscape architecture program, you can usually receive job assistance from the school's career services office. Although these services do not guarantee a job, they can be of great help in making initial contacts. Many positions are posted by the American Society of Landscape Architects and published in its two journals, *Landscape Architecture News Digest Online* (http://www. asla.org/members/land) and *Landscape Architecture* (http://www.

asla.org/nonmembers/lam.cfm). Government positions are normally filled through civil service examinations. Information regarding vacancies may be obtained through the local, state, or federal civil service commissions.

Most new hires are often referred to as interns or apprentices until they have gained initial experience in the field and have passed the necessary examinations. Apprentices' duties vary by employer; some handle background project research, others are directly involved in planning and design. Whatever their involvement, all new hires work under the direct supervision of a licensed landscape architect. All drawings and plans must be signed and sealed by the licensed supervisor for legal purposes.

ADVANCEMENT

After obtaining licensure and gaining work experience in all phases of a project's development, landscape architects can become project managers, responsible for overseeing the entire project and meeting schedule deadlines and budgets. They can also advance to the level of associate, increasing their earning opportunities by gaining a profitable stake in a firm.

The ultimate objective of many landscape architects is to gain the experience necessary to organize and open their own firm. According to the U.S. Department of Labor, approximately 25 percent of all landscape architects are self-employed—more than three times the average of workers in other professions. After the initial investment in computer-aided design software, few start-up costs are involved in breaking into the business independently.

EARNINGS

Salaries for landscape architects vary depending on the employer, work experience, location, and whether they are paid a straight salary or earn a percentage of a firm's profits.

According to 2006 data from the U.S. Department of Labor, the median annual salary for landscape architects was $55,140. The lowest paid 10 percent earned less than $34,230 and the highest paid 10 percent earned more than $95,420. The average salary for those working with the federal government in 2006 was $73,210.

Benefits also vary depending on the employer but usually include health insurance coverage, paid vacation time, and sick leave. Many landscape architects work for small landscaping firms or are self-employed. These workers generally receive fewer benefits than those who work for large organizations.

WORK ENVIRONMENT

Landscape architects spend much of their time in the field gathering information at the work site. They also spend time in the office, drafting plans and designs. Those working for larger organizations may have to travel farther away to worksites.

Work hours are generally regular, except during periods of increased business or when nearing a project deadline. Hours vary for self-employed workers because they determine their own schedules.

OUTLOOK

According to the *Occupational Outlook Handbook*, the employment of landscape architects is expected to increase faster than the average for all occupations through 2014. The increase in demand for landscape architects is a result of several factors: a boom in the construction industry, the need to refurbish existing sites, and the increase in city and environmental planning and historic preservation. In addition, many job openings are expected to result from the need to replace experienced workers who leave the field.

The need for landscape architecture depends to a great extent on the construction industry. In the event of an economic downturn, when real estate transactions and the construction business is expected to drop off, opportunities for landscape architects will also dwindle.

Opportunities will be the greatest for workers who develop strong technical skills. The growing use of technology such as computer-aided design will not diminish the demand for landscape architects. New and improved techniques will be used to create better designs more efficiently rather than reduce the number of workers needed to do the job.

FOR MORE INFORMATION

For information on the career, accredited education programs, licensure requirements, and available publications, contact
American Society of Landscape Architects
636 Eye Street, NW
Washington, DC 20001-3736

Tel: 202-898-2444
http://www.asla.org

For information on student resources, license examinations, and continuing education, contact
 Council of Landscape Architectural Registration Boards
 3949 Pender Drive, Suite 120
 Fairfax, VA 22030-6088
 Tel: 571-432-0332
 Email: Info@Clarb.org
 http://www.clarb.org

For career and educational information, visit the following Web site sponsored by the Landscape Architecture Foundation.
 LAprofession.org
 http://www.laprofession.org

INTERVIEW

Paul Miller is the owner of Paul Miller Design, Inc., a landscape architecture firm in Northfield, Minnesota, that specializes in golf course design. Since 1990 he has been involved in the design of more than 150 golf course projects. Paul discussed his career with the editors of Careers in Focus: Landscaping and Horticulture.

Q. How long have you been a landscape architect? Tell us about your business.

A. I have been a registered landscape architect since October 1990, after graduating with a bachelor's degree in landscape architecture from the University of Minnesota in 1987. My firm specializes in golf course architecture. I have designed golf courses throughout the United States but primarily my work is in the Midwest. Paul Miler Design, Inc., also offers landscape architecture and site planning.

Q. Why did you decide to become a landscape architect (and pursue a specialty in golf course design)?

A. I decided to pursue a career in landscape architecture because I loved the wide variety of skills that it encompasses, including art, science, and design. Golf course design is the best opportunity to use the skills that landscape architecture incorporates. Golf course architecture requires technical solutions that are artful and that create the setting for playing the game of golf.

It's a multilayered, problem-solving adventure every time you design a golf course.

Q. What do you like most and least about your career?

A. The best part of my job is having the freedom to shape the land to provide a dramatic landscape that people enjoy.

The worst parts of my job are the deadlines and the stress that comes when projects get behind schedule.

Q. What advice would you give to high school students who are interested in this career?

A. Art and science are great classes to take to gain the fundamental knowledge that landscape architecture encompasses. As you move into college, engineering, environmental studies, and computer skills will add to the skills that the field requires. Golf course architects should enjoy playing golf. Any experience gained in golf course construction or golf course maintenance will provide good learning experiences that relate directly to what golf course architects need to think about.

Traveling is a great opportunity to look at beautifully designed spaces that you can evaluate and decide what you like and don't like about them. Asking yourself how different spaces make you feel will start you thinking about how you go about designing spaces for public use. Other questions that put you in a design frame of mind would include asking yourself what materials were used and what construction techniques were needed? Experiencing your environment with this new way of looking at things will provide you with a new way of viewing the world you live in.

Q. What are the most important professional qualities for landscape architects?

A. Landscape architects should have great respect for the land and natural systems. They should be able to work with people in a collaborative environment to get projects completed. They need to have vision and passion for the process of designing outdoor spaces that will enrich the built environment.

Q. What is the future employment outlook in the field?

A. The future employment outlook for landscape architects is strong. With growing acknowledgement of the skills and leadership landscape architects bring to design projects, landscape architects continue to broaden the areas that they work in.

As people seek positive interactions with our environment the role of landscape architects will continue to move to the forefront. The need to address the environment with greater sensitivity to our impact makes the challenges of landscape architecture in the 21st century as important as any profession. It is a profession that rewards those who choose it with a sense of accomplishment and the ability to make a difference in the world that we inhabit.

Landscapers and Grounds Managers

QUICK FACTS

School Subjects
Biology
Chemistry

Personal Skills
Following instructions
Mechanical/manipulative

Work Environment
Primarily outdoors
Primarily multiple locations

Minimum Education Level
High school diploma

Salary Range
$21,260 to $37,300 to
$68,914+

Certification or Licensing
Required for certain
positions

Outlook
Faster than the average

DOT
408

GOE
03.01.02, 03.03.04

NOC
2225

O*NET-SOC
37-3011.00, 37-1012.00,
37-1012.01, 37-1012.02,
37-3013.00

OVERVIEW

Landscapers and *grounds managers* plan, design, and maintain gardens, parks, lawns, and other landscaped areas and supervise the care of the trees, plants, and shrubs that are part of these areas. Specific job responsibilities depend on the type of area involved. Landscapers and grounds managers direct projects at private homes, parks, schools, arboretums, office parks, shopping malls, government offices, and botanical gardens. They are responsible for purchasing material and supplies and for training, directing, and supervising employees. Grounds managers maintain the land after the landscaping designs have been implemented. They may work alone or supervise a grounds staff. They may have their own business or be employed by a landscaping firm. There are approximately 1.5 million grounds maintenance workers in the United States; about 184,000 of these workers are in management positions.

HISTORY

Landscaping formal gardens and cultivating flowers is artistic work. The hanging gardens of Babylon, the landscaped areas of Persia and India, and the smaller formal gardens of Athens are early examples of this art. In the 18th century, gardens became more informal and natural, as exemplified by the plantings around George Washington's Mount Vernon home.

The first large landscaped public area in the United States was New York's Central Park, created in the 1860s. While landscaped parks and gardens have not been as widespread in the United States as they have elsewhere, enthusiasm for them is growing as the population increases and people realize the importance of seeing natural beauty in their everyday surroundings.

THE JOB

There are many different types of landscapers and grounds managers, and their specific job titles depend on the duties involved. One specialist in this field is the *landscape contractor*, who performs landscaping work on a contract basis for homeowners, highway departments, operators of industrial parks, and others. They confer with prospective clients and study the landscape design, drawings, and bills of material to determine the amount of landscape work required. They plan the installation of lighting or sprinkler systems, erection of fences, and the types of trees, shrubs, and ornamental plants required. They inspect the grounds and calculate labor, equipment, and materials costs. They also prepare and submit bids, draw up contracts, and direct and coordinate the activities of landscape laborers who mow lawns, plant shrubbery, dig holes, move topsoil, and perform other related tasks.

Industrial-commercial grounds managers maintain areas in and around industrial or commercial properties by cutting lawns, pruning trees, raking leaves, and shoveling snow. They also plant grass and flowers and are responsible for the upkeep of flower beds and public passageways. These types of groundskeepers may repair and maintain fences and gates and also operate sprinkler systems and other equipment.

Parks-and-grounds managers maintain city, state, or national parks and playgrounds. They plant and prune trees; haul away garbage; repair driveways, walks, swings, and other equipment; and clean comfort stations.

Landscape supervisors supervise and direct the activities of landscape workers who are engaged in pruning trees and shrubs, caring for lawns, and performing related tasks. They coordinate work schedules, prepare job cost estimates, and deal with customer questions and concerns.

Landscapers maintain the grounds of private or business establishments. They care for hedges, gardens, and other landscaped areas. They mow and trim lawns, plant trees and shrubs, apply fertilizers and other chemicals, and repair walks and driveways.

Many *arboriculture technicians* work as landscapers or grounds managers. Below is a listing of some careers in this area.

Tree surgeons, sometimes known as *arborists*, prune and treat ornamental and shade trees to improve their health and appearance. This may involve climbing with ropes, working in buckets high off the ground, spraying fertilizers and pesticides, or injecting chemicals into the tree trunk or root zone in the ground. *Tree-trimming supervisors* coordinate and direct the activities of workers engaged in cutting away tree limbs or removing trees that interfere with electric power lines. They inspect power lines and direct the placement of removal equipment. Tree-trimming supervisors answer consumer questions when trees are located on private property.

Pest management scouts survey landscapes and nurseries regularly to locate potential pest problems including insects, diseases, and weeds before they become hard to control in an effective, safe manner. Scouts may specialize in the treatment of a particular type of infestation, such as gypsy moths or boll weevils.

Lawn-service workers plant and maintain lawns. They remove leaves and dead grass and apply insecticides, fertilizers, and weed killers as necessary. Lawn-service workers also use aerators and other tools to pierce the soil to make holes for the fertilizer and de-thatchers to remove built-up thatch.

Horticulturists conduct experiments and investigations into the problems of breeding, production, storage, processing, and transit of fruits, nuts, berries, flowers, and trees. They also develop new plant varieties and determine methods of planting, spraying, cultivating, and harvesting.

A *city forester* advises communities on the selection, planting schedules, and proper care of trees. They also plant, feed, spray, and prune trees and may supervise other workers in these activities. Depending on the situation, landscapers and groundskeepers may perform these functions alone or with city foresters.

Turfgrass consultants analyze turfgrass problems and recommend solutions. They also determine growing techniques, mowing schedules, and the best type of turfgrass to use for specified areas. Depending on the geographic area of the country, lawn-service companies regularly use such consultants.

On golf courses, landscapers and grounds managers are employed as *greenskeepers*. There are two types of greenskeepers: *greenskeepers I* supervise and coordinate the activities of workers engaged in keeping the grounds and turf of a golf course in good playing condition. They consult with the greens superintendent to plan and review work projects; they determine work assignments, such as fertilizing, irrigating, seeding, mowing, raking, and spraying; and they mix and prepare spraying and dusting solutions. They may also repair and maintain mechanical equipment.

Greenskeepers II follow the instructions of greenskeepers I as they maintain the grounds of golf courses. They cut the turf on green and tee areas; dig and rake grounds to prepare and cultivate new greens; connect hose and sprinkler systems; plant trees and shrubs; and operate tractors as they apply fertilizer, insecticide, and other substances to the fairways or other designated areas.

Greens superintendents, also known as *golf course superintendents*, supervise and coordinate the activities of greenskeepers and other workers engaged in constructing and maintaining golf course areas. They review test results of soil and turf samples, and they direct the application of fertilizer, lime, insecticide, or fungicide. Their other duties include monitoring the course grounds to determine the need for irrigation or better care, keeping and reviewing maintenance records, and interviewing and hiring workers.

REQUIREMENTS

High School

In general, a high school diploma is necessary for most positions, and at least some college training is needed for those with supervisory or specialized responsibilities. High school students interested in this career should take classes in English, mathematics, chemistry, biology, and as many courses as possible in horticulture and botany.

Postsecondary Training

Those interested in college training should enroll in a two- or four-year program in horticulture, landscape management, or agronomy. Classes might include landscape maintenance and design, turfgrass management, botany, and plant pathology. Course work should be selected with an area of specialization in mind. Those wishing to have managerial responsibilities should take courses in personnel management, communications, and business-related courses such as accounting and economics.

Many trade and vocational schools offer landscaping, horticulture, and related programs. Several extension programs are also available that allow students to take courses at home.

Certification or Licensing

Licensing and certification differ by state and vary according to specific job responsibilities. For example, in most states landscapers and grounds managers need a certificate to spray insecticides or other chemicals. Landscape contractors must be certified in some states.

Several professional associations offer certification programs for workers in the field. The Professional Grounds Management Society offers certification for both grounds managers and workers: the certified grounds manager (CGM) designation and the certified grounds technician (CGT) designation. The Professional Lawn Care Association of America offers the following designations to applicants who pass examinations: certified landscape professional; certified ornamental landscape professional; certified turfgrass professional; certified turfgrass professional, cool season lawns; certified landscape technician, interior; and certified landscape technician, exterior. The American Society for Horticultural Science offers the certified professional horticulturist designation.

Landscapers and grounds managers who specialize in the care of golf courses and sports fields can receive certification from the Golf Course Superintendents Association of America (GCSAA) or the Sports Turf Managers Association.

Contractors and other self-employed people may also need a license to operate their businesses.

Other Requirements

Aspiring landscapers and grounds managers should have "green thumbs," and an interest in preserving and maintaining natural areas. They should also be reasonably physically fit, have an aptitude for working with machines, and display good manual dexterity.

All managerial personnel must carefully supervise their workers to ensure that they adhere to environmental regulations as specified by the Environmental Protection Agency and other local and national government agencies.

EXPLORING

If you are between the ages of five and 22, you might want to join the National Junior Horticulture Association, which offers horticulture-related projects, contests, and other activities. Visit http://www.njha. org for more information.

Part-time work at a golf course, lawn-service company, greenhouse, botanical garden, or other similar enterprise is an excellent way of learning about this field. Many companies gladly hire part-time help, especially during the busy summer months. In addition, there are numerous opportunities mowing lawns, growing flowers, and tending gardens. You can also join garden clubs, visit local flower shops, and attend botanical shows.

Finally, a summer job mowing lawns and caring for a neighbor's garden is an easy, simple introduction to the field.

EMPLOYERS

Approximately 1.5 million grounds maintenance workers are employed in the United States. About 184,000 of these workers are in management positions. Landscapers and grounds managers are employed by golf courses, lawn-service companies, greenhouses, nurseries, botanical gardens, and public parks. Many people in this field start their own businesses.

STARTING OUT

Summer or part-time jobs often lead to full-time employment with the same employer. Those who enroll in a college or other training programs can receive help in finding work from the school's career services office. In addition, directly applying to botanical gardens, nurseries, or golf courses is common practice. Jobs may also be listed in newspaper want ads. Most landscaping and related companies provide on-the-job training for entry-level personnel.

ADVANCEMENT

In general, landscapers and grounds managers can expect to advance as they gain experience and additional educational training. For example, a greenskeeper with a high school diploma usually must have at least some college training to become a greens superintendent. It is also possible to go into a related field, such as selling equipment used in maintaining lawns and other natural areas.

Those in managerial positions may wish to advance to a larger establishment or go into consulting work. In some instances, skilled landscapers and grounds managers may start their own consulting or contracting businesses.

EARNINGS

Salaries depend on the experience and education level of the worker, the type of work being done, and geographic location. The U.S. Department of Labor reports the following median hourly earnings for workers in this industry in 2006: first-line supervisors/managers of landscaping, lawn service, and groundskeeping workers, $17.93 ($37,300 per year); tree trimmers and pruners, $13.58 ($28,250 per year); pesticide handlers, sprayers, and applicators, $12.84 ($26,700 per year); and landscaping and groundskeeping workers, $10.22 ($21,260 per year). Landscape contractors and others who run their own businesses earn between $25,000 and $50,000 per year, with those with a greater ability to locate customers earning even more. According to the Golf Course Superintendents Association of America, the average base salary for golf course superintendents was $68,914 in 2005.

Fringe benefits vary from employer to employer but generally include medical insurance and some paid vacation.

WORK ENVIRONMENT

Landscapers and grounds managers spend much of their time outside. Those with administrative or managerial responsibilities spend at least a portion of their workday in an office. Most of the outdoor work is done during daylight hours, but work takes place all year round in all types of weather conditions. Most people in the field work 37 to 40 hours a week, but overtime is especially likely during the summer months when landscapers and grounds managers take advantage of the longer days and warmer weather. Workweeks may be shorter during the winter. Weekend work is highly likely. Managerial personnel should be willing to work overtime updating financial records and making sure the business accounts are in order.

Much of the work can be physically demanding and most of it is performed outdoors in one extreme or another. Workers shovel dirt, trim bushes and trees, constantly bend down to plant flowers and shrubbery, and may have to climb ladders or the tree itself to prune branches or diagnose a problem. There is some risk of injury using planting and pruning machinery and some risk of illness from handling and breathing pesticides, but proper precautions should limit any job-related hazards.

OUTLOOK

Employment for this field is expected to grow faster than the average for all occupations through 2014, according to the *Occupational Outlook Handbook*. Landscapers and their services will be in strong demand due to increased construction of buildings, shopping malls, homes, and other structures. Upkeep and renovation of existing landscapes will create jobs as well. There is also a high degree of turnover in this field as many workers transfer to better-paying occupations, retire, or leave the field for other reasons.

Another factor for job growth is the increase in amount of disposable incomes. In order to have more leisure time, people are beginning to contract out for lawn care and maintenance. The popularity of home gardening will create jobs with local nurseries and garden centers. Jobs should be available with government agencies as well as in the private sector.

Nonseasonal work will be more prevalent in states such as California, Arizona, and Florida, where mild climates warrant landscaping and lawn maintenance year-round.

FOR MORE INFORMATION

For information on certification and training programs and to read the online publication Careers in Horticulture, *visit the ASHS Web site.*

American Society for Horticultural Science (ASHS)
113 South West Street, Suite 200
Alexandria, VA 22314-2851
Tel: 703-836-4606
http://www.ashs.org

For comprehensive information on golf course management careers, internships, job listings, turfgrass management programs, and certification, contact

Golf Course Superintendents Association of America
1421 Research Park Drive
Lawrence, KS 66049-3859
Tel: 800-472-7878
Email: infobox@gcsaa.org
http://www.gcsaa.org

For information on career opportunities and education, contact

Professional Grounds Management Society
720 Light Street
Baltimore, MD 21230-3816
Tel: 800-609-7467
Email: pgms@assnhqtrs.com
http://www.pgms.org

For information on careers and certification, contact
Professional Landcare Network
950 Herndon Parkway, Suite 450
Herndon, VA 20170-5528
Tel: 800-395-2522
http://www.landcarenetwork.org

For certification information, contact
Sports Turf Managers Association
805 New Hampshire, Suite E
Lawrence, KS 66044-2774
Tel: 800-323-3875
http://www.stma.org

For more information on arboriculture, contact
Tree Care Industry Association
Three Perimeter Road, Unit I
Manchester, NH 03103-3341
Tel: 800-733-2622
http://www.treecareindustry.org

For profiles of professionals working in a variety of careers, visit
enPlant: Horticulture & Crop Science in Virtual Perspective
http://enplant.osu.edu/index.lasso

Lawn and Gardening Service Owners

OVERVIEW

Lawn and gardening service owners maintain the lawns of residential and commercial properties. They cut grass and shrubbery, clean yards, and treat grass with fertilizer and insecticides. They may also landscape, which involves the arrangement of lawns, trees, and bushes. There are about 1.5 million people employed in the grounds maintenance industry. Approximately one out of every seven landscapers, groundskeepers, and nursery workers is self-employed.

HISTORY

If you've ever visited or seen photographs of the Taj Mahal in India or the Palace of Versailles in France, then you've seen some elaborate examples of the lawns and gardens of the world. For as long as people have built grand palaces, they have designed lawns and gardens to surround them. Private, irrigated gardens of ancient Egypt and Persia were regarded as paradise with their thick, green vegetation and cool shade. In the 16th century, Italians kept gardens that wound about fountains, columns, and steps. The English developed "cottage-style" gardens to adhere to the natural surroundings. Early American gardens, such as those surrounding Monticello in Virginia, were inspired by this English style.

The English also inspired the Georgian style of house design in the 18th century that caught on across Europe and America. Rows of houses down city blocks were designed as units, their yards

QUICK FACTS

School Subjects
Agriculture
Technical/shop

Personal Skills
Following instructions
Mechanical/manipulative

Work Environment
Primarily outdoors
Primarily multiple locations

Minimum Education Level
High school diploma

Salary Range
$23,940 to $50,000 to
$100,000+

Certification or Licensing
Voluntary (certification)
Required by certain states
(licensing)

Outlook
Faster than the average

DOT
408

GOE
03.01.02

NOC
N/A

O*NET-SOC
37-1012.00, 37-1012.01

hidden behind the houses and away from the streets. Lawn care as a business blossomed with the growth of population and home ownership between the Civil War and World War I. The sport of golf also became popular among the rich at this time, spurring further development of lawn care products and machinery. Since World War II, many people now hire lawn maintenance professionals to keep up and improve the look of their personal lawns and gardens.

THE JOB

Lawn and gardening businesses may choose to offer only a few services, such as lawn mowing and hedge clipping. But some businesses offer a large number of services, from simple cleaning to the actual design of the yard. Some lawn services specialize in organic lawn care. They rely on natural fertilizers and applications to control insects and lawn diseases instead of applying toxic chemicals to treat lawns.

When working for private homeowners, lawn and gardening services do yard work once or twice a week for each client. They arrive at the residence with equipment, such as a push or riding mower, an aerator, and a blower vac. Workers cut the grass and "weed-eat," trimming the weeds at the edges of the houses and fences. They also apply fertilizer and insecticide to the lawn to keep the grass healthy and use an aerator to run over the yard to make holes in the topsoil and allow more airflow.

Lawn and gardening service owners participate in all aspects of the business, including the labor. They plant grass seed in areas where there is little growth, and use blowers to blow leaves and other debris from the yard, sidewalks, and driveway. Lawn services are often called in after storms and other natural disasters to clean up and repair lawns.

"There are a lot of little services you can throw in to keep you busy," says Sam Morgan, who operates a lawn care service in Dallas, Texas. He does general lawn maintenance for residential yards and some rental properties. "Having some rental property can be good," he says. "It's year-round work. But it can also be dirty work; you have to pick up a lot of trash."

In addition to mowing yards and weed-eating, he assists with planting flower beds, cleaning house gutters, and some light tree work. Tree care involves the pruning and trimming of branches. Lawn and gardening services may need to remove dead or unwanted trees before planting new ones. They may also offer landscaping services, offering advice on arranging the lawn. Service owners assist in positioning trees, bushes, fountains, flower beds, and lighting. They may also put up wood or metal fencing, and install sprinkler systems.

"I started the business on a shoestring," Morgan says. "But I learned early that you have to have good equipment." He now owns a commercial mower that can handle 200 yards a week.

Lawn and gardening service owners have other responsibilities than just lawn and garden care. As owners, they are responsible for the business end of the service. In order to stay in business, owners must balance the budget, collect on accounts, repair or replace equipment when necessary, order supplies, and, depending on the size of the business, may hire and manage other employees.

In addition to working on the demanding yard work, Morgan spends much of his time attending to business details, such as keeping tax records, making phone calls, and preparing estimates and bills.

REQUIREMENTS

High School

Take agriculture, shop, and other courses that will help you gain familiarity with the machinery, fertilizers, and chemicals used in lawn maintenance. Agriculture courses will also teach you about different grasses and plants, and how to care for them. Joining associations such as the National FFA Organization (formerly the Future Farmers of America) and 4-H can give you additional experience with horticulture. Business and accounting courses are also useful to learn about record keeping, budgeting, and finances.

Postsecondary Training

After high school, you can learn about lawn maintenance on the job, either by assisting someone with an established lawn care business, or by taking on a few residential customers yourself. Though a college degree is not necessary, lawn and gardening service owners benefit from advanced courses such as small business management and finance to help run their business.

Certification or Licensing

Certification is not required, but many lawn and garden service owners choose to earn professional certifications from the Professional Landcare Network. The network offers the following certification designations: certified landscape professional, certified landscape technician–interior, certified landscape technician–exterior, certified turfgrass professional, certified turfgrass professional–cool season lawns, and certified ornamental landscape professional. Depending on the certification, applicants must pass a multiple-choice examination or a hands-on field test.

Most states require lawn care professionals who apply pesticides to be licensed. This usually involves passing a written examination on the safe use and disposal of toxic chemicals.

Other Requirements

As entrepreneurs, lawn and gardening service owners need to have people skills and be self-motivated to successfully promote their own business and attract clients.

"I'm a good salesman," Sam Morgan says. He also emphasizes the need to be committed to doing a quality job for every customer. Service owners should have an eye for detail to notice all the areas where lawns need work. They must also be in fairly good health to withstand the hard labor that the job calls for, often during the heat of the summer.

EXPLORING

If you've made some extra money mowing lawns for your neighbors, then you're already familiar with many of the aspects of a lawn care service. Walking behind a power mower during the hottest days of the year may make you miserable, but early experience in keeping your next-door neighbor's lawn looking nice is a great opportunity for self-employment. Other sources for potential clients are private homeowners, apartment complex communities, golf courses, and parks. Look into volunteer and part-time work with botanical gardens, greenhouses, and park and recreation crews.

Opportunities to learn how to care for a lawn and garden are no further than your own backyard. Experiment with planting and maintaining different varieties of flowers, shrubs, or trees. Chances are, you'll gain valuable experience and your parents will thank you!

In addition to getting dirt under your fingernails, you can also explore the lawn and garden services by reading magazines and books on lawn and garden care. Cable television stations, such as Home and Garden Television (HGTV), feature programming about gardening.

Every summer, many high school students find reliable work mowing lawns. But many of these students tire of the work early in the summer. Be persistent in seeking out work all summer long.

You should also be committed to doing good work; you'll have stiff competition from professional lawn care businesses that offer more services, own commercial machinery, and have extensive knowledge of fertilizers and pesticides. Some lawn care companies also hire students for summer work.

EMPLOYERS

Lawn and gardening service owners work primarily for private homeowners, though they may also contract work with commercial properties. Condos, hotels, apartment complexes, golf courses, sports fields, and parks all require regular lawn service.

Owners who choose to build their own business face challenges such as covering the costs of start up and establishing a client base. To defray these costs and risks, many choose to purchase and operate an existing business. There are a number of franchise opportunities in lawn care that, for a fee, will assist you in promoting your business and building a clientele. Emerald Green Lawn Care, Liqui-Green Lawn Care, and Lawn Doctor are just a few. NaturaLawn of America is a franchise that provides organic-based lawn care.

STARTING OUT

Most lawn and gardening service owners start out working for established services and work their way into positions of management or higher responsibility. A typical entry-level job is that of the landscape service technician. After a few years on the job, promising technicians may be promoted to supervisor positions such as regional or branch managers. According to the Professional Landcare Network, "Once a supervisory position is reached, leadership is the key to success." Workers who are organized, show strong leadership, and can make decisions quickly and wisely will have the best chances for promotion and may choose to start up their own business.

However, not all service owners follow this route. Sam Morgan's lawn service was not his first venture into entrepreneurship; he had once owned a number of dry cleaners. After selling the dry cleaners, he went to work for a chemical company. When the company downsized, Morgan was faced with finding a new job. He decided to turn to lawn care.

"I just went to Sears and bought a mower," he says. Since then, he's been able to invest in commercial machinery that can better handle the demands of the work, and he's found a number of ways to increase business. "I bill once a month," he says. "I get more business that way." He's also expanding his service to include some light landscaping, such as shrub work and planting small trees.

Depending on the business, start-up costs can vary. To purchase commercial quality equipment, the initial investment can be between $3,000 and $4,000. To buy into a franchise, however, will cost thousands of dollars more.

ADVANCEMENT

Once lawn and gardening service owners establish their own businesses, advancement can come in the form of expanded services. Some lawn professionals offer equipment and supply sales. With extended services, owners can reach out to a larger body of clients, securing larger contracts with golf courses, cities and local communities, and sports teams.

Sam Morgan currently has one employee, but he hopes for his business to grow more, allowing him to hire others. "I don't want to be doing so much of the physical work," he says.

With additional education, owners can also advance into other areas of lawn care and become contractors or landscape architects.

EARNINGS

Earnings in lawn care depend on a number of factors, such as geographic location, the size of the business, and the level of experience. Lawn care services generally make more money in areas of the country that have mild winters, offering more months of lawn growth and, as a result, requiring more care. The size of the client base also greatly affects earnings. A lawn care professional with a small clientele may make less than $20,000 a year, while the owner of a franchise lawn care company with a number of contracts and a large staff can make over $100,000.

According to 2006 data from the U.S. Department of Labor, first-line supervisors/managers of landscaping, lawn service, and grounds-keeping workers made an average of $17.93 an hour (or $37,300 annually). Salaries ranged from less than $23,940 to $60,930 or more annually. The Professional Landcare Network offers the following summary of earnings potential for management positions: first-level supervisors, $35,000; branch managers, $50,000 or more; regional managers, $60,000s; and successful owners, $100,000 or more.

WORK ENVIRONMENT

To many, working on a lawn or garden is relaxing, and the opportunity to work outdoors during pleasant days of spring and summer is enjoyable. However, the work can also be exhausting and strenuous. Lawn and gardening service owners fully involved in the labor of the business may have to lift heavy equipment from trucks, climb trees, and do a lot of walking, kneeling, and bending on the job. Depending on the nature of the business, service owners may have to exercise caution when handling harmful chemicals used in pesticides. In addition, they have to deal with a loud work environment because machinery such as lawn mowers, weed eaters, and blower vacs can be very noisy.

One benefit of owning a business is the ability to create a flexible work schedule. "Most likely," Sam Morgan says, "during the spring and summer, you can make plenty of money. There's plenty of work to be done." But some of that work may be in the hottest days of the summer, or on rainy days. With your own service, you can arrange to work regular weekday hours, or you can schedule weekends.

OUTLOOK

The benefits of a nice lawn aren't just aesthetic; a well-kept lawn can increase property value and provide a safe place for children to play. According to the National Gardening Association, more than 34 million U.S. households spent $44.7 billion on professional lawn and landscape services in 2006, up from 23.8 million households and $24.5 billion in 2001.

This spending promises a good future for lawn care services. The sale of lawn care products is expected to grow as more houses are built and more people recognize the importance of quality lawn care. The Environmental Protection Agency promotes the environmental benefits of a healthy lawn, emphasizing that healthy grass is not only attractive, but controls dust and pollens, provides oxygen, and improves the quality of groundwater. More people now recognize that a nice lawn can increase home value by as much as 20 percent, according to studies.

Technological developments will also aid the industry. With better, more economical equipment, lawn care professionals can do more specialized work in less time, allowing them to keep their service fees low.

FOR MORE INFORMATION

For general information about franchising, specific franchise opportunities, and to read the Franchise Opportunities Guide, *contact the IFA.*
International Franchise Association (IFA)
1501 K Street, NW, Suite 350
Washington, DC 20005-1412
Tel: 202-628-8000
http://www.franchise.org

To further explore the agriculture industry and for information on student chapters, contact
National FFA Organization
6060 FFA Drive
PO Box 68960
Indianapolis, IN 46268-0960
Tel: 317-802-6060
http://www.ffa.org

For information on certification, careers, internships, and student membership, contact
Professional Landcare Network
950 Herndon Parkway, Suite 450
Herndon, VA 20170-5528
Tel: 800-395-2522
http://www.landcarenetwork.org/cms/home.html

Nursery Owners and Managers

OVERVIEW

Nursery owners and managers are responsible for all aspects of the operation of a nursery, garden center, or greenhouse—from growing, feeding, transplanting, and protecting plants to overseeing day-to-day operations (including sales, marketing, human resources, customer relations, building upkeep, and accounting).

HISTORY

Robert Prince established the Prince Nursery in Flushing, New York, in 1737. It was the first commercial plant nursery in the United States. The nursery was so popular that it was even visited by President George Washington in 1789. During its approximately 150-year operation, it was known as one of the top nurseries in the United States.

The American Nursery & Landscape Association, the leading trade association of the nursery and landscape industry, was founded in 1876. It continues to represent the needs of the industry today.

Today, commercial nurseries, greenhouses, and garden centers, both small and large, can be found throughout the United States.

THE JOB

Owners and managers are responsible for the operation of nurseries, garden centers, and greenhouses.

Many nurseries grow their own stock, but at times owners and managers must order more exotic plants from other vendors. Owners and managers work with a budget that includes the cost of growing seedlings in their greenhouses, as well as purchasing plants from other vendors. They may use past sales records, information on new trends in gardening, and marketing research to determine the types and quantities of plants grown and sold at the store.

Nursery workers inspect probes used to measure soil temperature and soil moisture content. (*Stephen Ausmus, Agricultural Research Service, U.S. Department of Agriculture*)

In addition, owners and managers oversee the process of preparing plants for sale. They work with horticultural technicians to identify and avoid any potential problems with plants such as pests, disease, and inclement weather, as well as monitor proper watering and fertilizing techniques.

Owners and managers also provide customer service. They answer questions regarding the care of trees, shrubs, or grass; the type of soil and fertilizer to use; and countless other topics. They address customer complaints in a positive manner that will encourage the customer to return to make future purchases.

An important duty of owners and managers is employee relations. They interview, hire, and train new employees to work in various aspects of the business. These include technicians, laborers, and groundskeepers who work directly with the plants, and sales workers and landscape designers who deal directly with customers. Owners and managers create work schedules, assign duties to employees, and monitor work performance.

In both large and small operations, nursery owners and managers must keep up to date on product information (such as new plant hybrids, types of potting soil, or garden tools), as well as on economic and technological conditions that may have an impact on business. This entails reading catalogs about product availability, checking current inventories and prices, and researching and implementing any technological advances that may make the operation more efficient. For example, an owner may decide to purchase an automatic watering system that will reduce the amount of employee hours spent on this time-consuming task.

Owners and managers also have bookkeeping and accounting duties. They must keep records of payroll, taxes, and money spent and received.

If the nursery is part of a chain, the store manager reports to a district or regional manager. In the case of a single unit, or family-run establishment, then the manager reports directly to the owner.

REQUIREMENTS

High School

A high school diploma is important in order to understand the basics of business ownership and management, though there are no specific educational or experiential requirements for this position. Course work in business administration is helpful, as is previous experience in the retail trade. Hard work, constant analysis and evaluation, and sufficient capital are important elements of a successful business venture.

If you are interested in owning or managing a business, you should take courses in mathematics, business management, and in business-related subjects, such as accounting, typing, and computer science. In addition, pursue English and other courses that enhance your communications skills. Specific skill areas also should be developed. For example, if you want to own or manage a nursery, you should learn as much about horticulture as possible.

Owners of small retail businesses often manage the store and work behind the counter. In such a case, the owner of a nursery may wear many hats, acting as the horticultural technician, laborer, and landscape designer, as well.

Postsecondary Training

As the business environment gets more and more competitive, many people are opting for an academic degree as a way of getting more training. A bachelor's program emphasizing business communications, marketing, business law, business management, and accounting should be pursued. Some people choose to get a master's in business administration or other related graduate degree. There are also special business schools that offer one- or two-year programs in business management. Some correspondence schools also offer courses on how to plan and run a business. If you are interested in owning or managing a nursery or garden center, it is important that you take courses or earn a degree in horticulture or a related field.

Certification or Licensing

A business license may be required by some states. Individual states or communities may have zoning codes or other regulations specifying what type of business can be located in a particular area. Check with your state's chamber of commerce or department of revenue for more information on obtaining a license, or visit http://www. sba.gov/hotlist/license.html.

Other Requirements

Whatever the experience and training, a nursery owner needs a lot of energy, patience, and fortitude to overcome the slow times and other difficulties involved in running a business. Other important personal characteristics include maturity, creativity, and good business judgment. Nursery owners also should be able to motivate employees and delegate authority.

To be a successful nursery manager, you should have good communication skills, enjoy working with and supervising people, and be willing to put in very long hours. Diplomacy often is necessary when creating schedules for workers and in disciplinary matters. There is a great deal of responsibility in retail management and such positions often are stressful. A calm disposition and ability to handle stress will serve you well. You should also be in good physical shape since you will occasionally help your employees lift or rearrange plants, trees, gardening tools, and other products.

EXPLORING

A full- or part-time job as a sales clerk or in some other capacity at a nursery or garden center is a good way to learn about the responsibilities of operating such a business. Talking with owners of nurseries and garden centers is also helpful, as is reading periodicals that publish articles on self-employment, such as *Entrepreneur* magazine (http://www.entrepreneur.com).

Most communities have a chamber of commerce whose members usually will be glad to share their insights into the career of a retail business owner. The Small Business Administration, an agency of the U.S. government, is another possible source of information.

EMPLOYERS

Nurseries and garden centers are located throughout the nation. Many of these establishments are family owned. Members of younger generations are trained in the business of providing gardening and landscaping products and services, eventually becoming managers and owners of the company. Employment can also be obtained at nationwide home improvement chains such as Home Depot, Menard's, and Lowe's. Skilled and knowledgeable managers are needed to run the stores' year-round garden and nursery departments.

STARTING OUT

Few people start their career as a nursery owner or manager. Many people enter the industry by working as horticultural technicians, sales workers, designers, or assistant managers. Once they gain enough experience, they may be promoted to managerial positions. Others, especially those with advanced degrees, may start at the managerial level, or may opt to invest in their own business.

Owning a franchise is another way of starting a business without a large capital investment, as franchise agreements often involve some assistance in planning and start-up costs. Franchise operations, however, are not necessarily less expensive to run than a totally independent business.

ADVANCEMENT

Because a nursery owner is by definition the boss, there are limited opportunities for advancement. Advancement often takes the form of expansion of an existing business, leading to increased earnings and prestige. Expanding a business also can entail added risk, as it involves increasing operational costs. A successful franchise owner may be offered an additional franchise location or an executive position at the corporate headquarters. Some owners become part-time consultants, while others teach a course at a college or university or in an adult education program. This teaching often is done not only for the financial rewards but also as a way of helping others investigate the option of retail ownership.

Advancement opportunities for nursery managers in the horticultural retail industry vary according to the size of the store, where the store is located, and the type of merchandise sold. Advancement also depends on the individual's work experience and educational background. A store manager who works for a large retail chain, such as Home Depot, for example, may be given responsibility for the garden department in a number of stores in a given area or region or transferred to a larger store in another city. Willingness to relocate to a new city may increase an employee's promotional opportunities.

Some nursery managers decide to open their own stores after they have acquired enough experience in the industry. After working as a retail manager for a large chain of garden stores, for example, a person may decide to open a small store specializing in exotic plants or open a landscaping business.

EARNINGS

Earnings vary widely and are greatly influenced by the ability of the individual owner, the type of product or service being sold, and existing economic conditions. Some retail nursery owners may earn less than $15,000 a year, while the most successful owners earn $200,000 or more.

According to the U.S. Department of Labor, median annual earnings of agricultural managers (including those who manage nurseries and greenhouses) were $52,070 in 2006. Salaries ranged from less than $29,760 to more than $100,050 per year. Managers who oversee an entire region for a retail chain can earn more than $125,000. In addition to a salary, some stores offer their managers special bonuses, or commissions, which are typically connected to the store's performance. Many stores also offer employee discounts on store merchandise.

WORK ENVIRONMENT

Nurseries and garden centers are usually pleasant places to work. Managers and owners work indoors in comfortable office and outdoors in greenhouses and sales areas amidst a variety of beautiful plants, shrubs, and trees. People who are allergic to certain plants, pesticides, chemical sprays, or fertilizers should carefully consider choosing employment in this field.

Ownership is a demanding occupation, with owners often working six or seven days a week. Working more than 60 hours a week is not unusual, especially between March and September in most regions (when most plants and horticulture-related services are purchased) and other busy times. An owner of a large establishment may be able to leave a manager in charge of many parts of the business, but the owner still must be available to solve any pressing concerns. Owners of small businesses often stay in the store throughout the day, spending much of the time on their feet.

OUTLOOK

The nursery and greenhouse industry is the fastest growing segment of the U.S. agriculture industry, according to the U.S. Department of Agriculture. The nursery industry is a major provider of jobs and had sales of approximately $16 billion in 2005. As a result, opportunities should be good for nursery owners and managers over the next decade.

The retail field is extremely competitive, and many businesses fail each year. The most common reason for failure is poor management. Thus people with some managerial experience or training will likely have the best chance at running or owning a successful nursery.

FOR MORE INFORMATION

For industry information, contact
American Nursery & Landscape Association
1000 Vermont Avenue, NW, Suite 300
Washington, DC 20005-4914

Tel: 202-789-2900
http://www.anla.org

For more information on nursery management careers and student programs, contact
National FFA Organization
6060 FFA Drive
PO Box 68960
Indianapolis, IN 46268-0960
Tel: 317-802-6060
http://www.ffa.org

For materials on educational programs in the retail industry, contact
National Retail Federation
325 Seventh Street, NW, Suite 1100
Washington, DC 20004-2818
Tel: 800-673-4692
http://www.nrf.com

For a business starter packet with information about its loan program and services, and basic facts about starting a business, contact
U.S. Small Business Administration
6302 Fairview Road, Suite 300
Charlotte, NC 28210-0001
Tel: 800-827-5722
Email: answerdesk@sba.gov
http://www.sbaonline.sba.gov

Soil Conservationists and Technicians

OVERVIEW

Soil conservationists develop conservation plans to help farmers and ranchers, developers, homeowners, and government officials best use their land while adhering to government conservation regulations. They suggest plans to conserve and reclaim soil, preserve or restore wetlands and other rare ecological areas, rotate crops for increased yields and soil conservation, reduce water pollution, and restore or increase wildlife populations. They assess land users' needs, costs, maintenance requirements, and the life expectancy of various conservation practices. They plan design specifications using survey and field information, technical guides, and engineering field manuals. Soil conservationists also give talks to various organizations to educate land users and the public about how to conserve and restore soil and water resources. Many of their recommendations are based on information provided to them by soil scientists.

Soil conservation technicians work more directly with land users by putting the ideas and plans of the conservationist into action. In their work they use basic engineering and surveying tools, instruments, and techniques. They perform engineering surveys and design and implement conservation practices like terraces and grassed waterways. Soil conservation technicians monitor projects during and after construction and periodically revisit the site to evaluate the practices and plans.

HISTORY

In 1908, President Theodore Roosevelt appointed a National Conservation Commission to oversee the proper conservation of the country's natural resources. As a result, many state and local conservation organizations were formed, and Americans began to take a serious interest in preserving their land's natural resources.

Despite this interest, however, conservation methods were not always understood or implemented. For example, farmers in the southern Great Plains, wanting to harvest a cash crop, planted many thousands of acres of wheat during the early decades of the 20th century. The crop was repeated year after year until the natural grasslands of the area were destroyed and the soil was depleted of nutrients. When the area experienced prolonged droughts combined with the naturally occurring high winds, devastating dust storms swept the land during the 1930s. Parts of Oklahoma, Texas, Kansas, New Mexico, and Colorado suffered from severe soil erosion that resulted in desert-like conditions, and this ruined area became known as the Dust Bowl.

As a result of what happened to the Dust Bowl, Congress established the Natural Resources Conservation Service of the U.S. Department of Agriculture in 1935. Because more than 800 million tons of topsoil had already been blown away by the winds over the plains, the job of reclaiming the land through wise conservation practices was not an easy one. In addition to the large areas of the Great Plains that had become desert land, there were other badly eroded lands throughout the country.

Fortunately, emergency planning came to the aid of the newly established conservation program. The Civilian Conservation Corps (CCC) was created to help alleviate unemployment during the Great Depression of the 1930s. The CCC established camps in rural areas and assigned people to aid in many different kinds of conservation. Soil conservationists directed those portions of the CCC program designed to halt the loss of topsoil by wind and water action.

Much progress has been made in the years since the Natural Resources Conservation Service was established. Wasted land has been reclaimed and further loss has been prevented. Land-grant colleges have initiated programs to help farmers understand the principles and procedures of soil conservation. The Cooperative Research, Education, and Extension Service (within the Department of Agriculture) provides workers who are skilled in soil conservation to work with these programs.

Throughout the United States today there are several thousand federally appointed soil conservation districts. A worker employed by the government works in these districts to demonstrate soil conservation to farmers and agricultural businesses. There are usually one or more professional soil conservationists and one or more soil conservation technicians working in each district.

THE JOB

Soil sustains plant and animal life, influences water and air quality, and supports human health and habitation. Its quality has a major impact on ecological balance, biological diversity, air quality, water flow, and plant growth, including crops and forestation. Soil conservationists and technicians help scientists and engineers collect samples and data to determine soil quality, identify problems, and develop plans to better manage the land. They work with farmers, agricultural professionals, landowners, range managers, and public and private agencies to establish and maintain sound conservation practices.

A farmer or landowner contacts soil conservationists to help identify soil quality problems, improve soil quality, maintain it, or stop or reverse soil degradation. Conservationists visit the site to gather information, beginning with past and current uses of the soil and future plans for the site. They consult precipitation and soil maps and try to determine if the way land is being currently used is somehow degrading the soil quality. Conservationists consider irrigation practices, fertilizer use, and tillage systems. At least a five- to 10-year history of land use is most helpful for working in this field.

Site observation reveals signs of soil quality problems. The farmer or landowner can point out areas of concern that occur regularly, such as wet spots, salt accumulation, rills and gullies, or excessive runoff water that could indicate erosion, stunted plant growth, or low crop yield. Samples are taken from these areas and tested for such physical, chemical, and biological properties as soil fertility, soil structure, soil stability, water storage and availability, and nutrient retention. Conservationists also look at plant characteristics, such as rooting depth, which can indicate density or compaction of the soil.

Once all the data are gathered and samples tested, conservationists analyze the results. They look for patterns and trends. If necessary, they take additional samples to verify discrepancies or confirm results. They prepare a report for the farmer or landowner.

A team of conservationists, engineers, scientists, and the landowners propose alternative solutions for soil problems. All the alternatives must be weighed carefully for their possible effects on ecological balance, natural resources, economic factors, and social or cultural factors. The landowner makes the final decision on which solutions to use and a plan is drafted.

After the plan is in place, soil conservationists and technicians continue to monitor and evaluate soil conditions, usually over a period of several years. Periodic soil sampling shows whether progress is being made, and if not, changes can be made to the plan.

These brief examples show how the process works. A farmer has a problem with crop disease. He sees that the yield is reduced and the health of his plants is poor. Soil conservationists and technicians consider possible causes and test soil for pests, nutrient deficiencies, lack of biological diversity, saturated soil, and compacted layers. Depending on test results, conservationists might suggest a pest-management program, an improved drainage system, the use of animal manure, or crop rotation.

Another farmer notices the formation of rills and gullies on his land along with a thinning topsoil layer. Soil conservationists' research shows that the erosion is due to such factors as lack of cover, excessive tillage that moves soil down a slope, intensive crop rotation, and low organic matter. Suggested solutions include reducing tillage, using animal manure, planting cover crops or strip crops, and using windbreaks.

Conservationists and technicians who work for the Bureau of Land Management, which oversees hundreds of millions of acres of public domain, help survey publicly owned areas and pinpoint land features to determine the best use of public lands. Soil conservation technicians working in the Bureau of Reclamation assist civil, construction, materials, or general engineers. Their job is to oversee certain phases of such projects as the construction of dams and irrigation planning. The Bureau's ultimate goal is the control of water and soil resources for the benefit of farms, homes, and cities.

Other soil conservationists and technicians work as *range technicians*, who help determine the value of rangeland, its grazing capabilities, erosion hazards, and livestock potential. *Physical science technicians* gather data in the field, studying the physical characteristics of the soil, make routine chemical analyses, and set up and operate test apparatus. *Cartographic survey technicians* work with *cartographers* (mapmakers) to map or chart the earth or graphically represent geographical information, survey the public domain, set boundaries, pinpoint land features, and determine the most beneficial public use. *Engineering technicians* conduct field tests and oversee some phases of construction on dams and irrigation projects. They also measure acreage, place property boundaries, and define drainage areas on maps. *Surveying technicians* perform surveys for field measurement and mapping, to plan for construction, to check the accuracy of dredging operations, or to provide reference points and lines for related work. They gather data for the design and construction of highways, dams, topographic maps, and nautical or aeronautical charts.

REQUIREMENTS

High School

While in high school, you should take at least one year each of algebra, geometry, and trigonometry. Take several years of English to develop your writing, research, and speaking skills as these are skills you will need when compiling reports and working with others. Science classes, of course, are important to take, including earth science, biology, and chemistry. If your high school offers agriculture classes, be sure to take any relating to land use, crop production, and soils.

Postsecondary Training

Conservationists hold bachelor's degrees in areas such as general agriculture, range management, crop or soil science, forestry, and agricultural engineering. Teaching and research positions require further graduate level education in a natural resources field. Though government jobs do not necessarily require a college degree (a combination of appropriate experience and education can serve as a substitute), a college education can make you more desirable for a position.

Typical beginning courses include applied mathematics, communication skills, basic soils, botany, chemistry, zoology, and introduction to range management. Advanced courses include American government, surveying, forestry, game management, soil and water conservation, economics, fish management, and conservation engineering.

Conservationists and technicians must have some practical experience in the use of soil conservation techniques before they enter the field. Many schools require students to work in the field during the school year or during summer vacation before they can be awarded their degree. Jobs are available in the federal park systems and with privately owned industries.

Certification or Licensing

No certification or license is required of soil conservationists and technicians; however, becoming certified can improve your skills and professional standing. The American Society of Agronomy offers voluntary certification in soil science/classification.

Most government agencies require applicants to take a competitive examination for consideration.

Other Requirements

Soil conservationists and technicians must be able to apply practical as well as theoretical knowledge to their work. You must have a working knowledge of soil and water characteristics; be skilled in management of woodlands, wildlife areas, and recreation areas; and have knowledge of surveying instruments and practices, mapping, and the procedures used for interpreting aerial photographs.

Soil conservationists and technicians should also be able to write clear, concise reports to demonstrate and explain the results of tests, studies, and recommendations. A love for the outdoors and an appreciation for all natural resources are essential for success and personal fulfillment in this job.

EXPLORING

One of the best ways to become acquainted with soil conservation work and technology is through summer or part-time work on a farm or at a natural park. Other ways to explore this career include joining a local chapter of the 4-H Club or National FFA Organization (formerly Future Farmers of America). Science courses that include lab sections and mathematics courses focusing on practical problem solving will also help give you a feel for this kind of work.

EMPLOYERS

Nearly two-thirds of all conservation workers are employed by local and federal government agencies. At the federal level, most soil conservationists and technicians work for the Natural Resources Conservation Service, the Bureau of Land Management, and the Bureau of Reclamation. Others work for agencies at the state and county level. Soil conservationists and technicians also work for private agencies and firms such as banks and loan agencies, mining or steel companies, and public utilities. A small percentage of workers are self-employed consultants who advise private industry owners and government agencies.

STARTING OUT

Most students gain outside experience by working a summer job in their area of interest. You can get information on summer positions through your school's career services office. Often, contacts made on summer jobs lead to permanent employment after graduation. College career counselors and faculty members are often valuable sources of advice and information on finding employment.

Most soil conservationists and technicians find work with state, county, or federal agencies. Hiring procedures for these jobs vary according to the level of government in which the applicant is seeking work. In general, however, students begin the application procedure during the fourth semester of their program and take some form of competitive examination as part of the process. College career services personnel can help students find out about the application procedures. Representatives of government agencies often visit college campuses to explain employment opportunities to students and sometimes to recruit for their agencies.

ADVANCEMENT

Soil conservationists and technicians usually start out with a local conservation district to gain experience and expertise before advancing to the state, regional, or national level.

In many cases, conservationists and technicians continue their education while working by taking evening courses at a local college or technical institute. Federal agencies that employ conservationists and technicians have a policy of promotion from within. Because of this policy, there is a continuing opportunity for such workers to advance through the ranks. The degree of advancement that all conservationists and technicians can expect in their working careers is determined by their aptitudes, abilities, and, of course, their desire to advance.

Workers seeking a more dramatic change can transfer their skills to related jobs outside the conservation industry, such as farming or land appraisal.

EARNINGS

The majority of soil conservationists and technicians work for the federal government, and their salaries are determined by their government service rating. In 2005, the average annual salary for soil conservationists was $53,350. Those employed by the federal government had an average annual salary of $60,671, according to the *Occupational Outlook Handbook*. Starting salaries for those with bachelor's degrees employed by the federal government was $24,677 or $30,567 in 2005, depending on academic achievement. Those with master's degrees earned a higher starting salary of $37,390 or $45,239, and with a doctorate, $54,221.

The U.S. Department of Labor reports that median earnings for soil and plant scientists were $56,080 in 2006. Some scientists earned less than $33,650, while others earned $93,460 or more annually.

The U.S. Department of Labor reports that median earnings for forest and conservation technicians (including those who specialize in soil science) were $30,880 in 2006. Salaries ranged from less than $22,450 to more than $49,380 annually.

The salaries of conservationists and technicians working for private firms or agencies are roughly comparable to those paid by the federal government. Earnings at the state and local levels vary depending on the region but are typically lower.

Government jobs and larger private industries offer comprehensive benefit packages that are usually more generous than those offered at smaller firms.

WORK ENVIRONMENT

Soil conservationists and technicians usually work 40 hours per week except in unusual or emergency situations. They have opportunities to travel, especially when they work for federal agencies.

Soil conservation is an outdoor job. Workers travel to work sites by car but must often walk great distances to an assigned area. Although they sometimes work from aerial photographs and other on-site pictures, they cannot work from pictures alone. They must visit the spot that presents the problem in order to make appropriate recommendations.

Although soil conservationists and technicians spend much of their working time outdoors, indoor work is also necessary when generating detailed reports of their work to agency offices.

In their role as assistants to professionals, soil conservation technicians often assume the role of government public relations representatives when dealing with landowners and land managers. They must be able to explain the underlying principles of the structures that they design and the surveys that they perform.

To meet these and other requirements of the job, conservationists and technicians should be prepared to continue their education both formally and informally throughout their careers. They must stay aware of current periodicals and studies so that they can keep up-to-date in their areas of specialization.

Soil conservationists and technicians gain satisfaction from knowing that their work is vitally important to the nation's economy and environment. Without their expertise, large portions of land in the United States could become barren within a generation.

OUTLOOK

The U.S. Department of Labor predicts employment for conservation scientists (a category including soil conservationists) to grow slower than the average for all occupations through 2014, mainly due to decreased federal spending in this area. Nevertheless, the need for government involvement in protecting natural resources should remain strong. More opportunities may be available with state and local government agencies, which are aware of needs in their areas. The vast majority of America's cropland has suffered from some sort of erosion, and only continued efforts by soil conservation professionals can prevent a dangerous depletion of our most valuable resource: fertile soil.

Some soil conservationists and technicians are employed as research and testing experts for public utility companies, banks and loan agencies, and mining or steel companies. At present, a relatively small number of soil conservation workers are employed by these firms or agencies. However, it is these private-sector areas that will provide the most employment opportunities over the next 10 years.

FOR MORE INFORMATION

For information on soil conservation careers and certification, contact

American Society of Agronomy
677 South Segoe Road
Madison, WI 53711-1086
Tel: 608-273-8080
Email: headquarters@agronomy.org
http://www.agronomy.org

For information on seminars, issues affecting soil scientists, and educational institutions offering soil science programs, contact

National Society of Consulting Soil Scientists
PO Box 1724
Sandpoint, ID 83864-0901

Tel: 800-535-7148
Email: info2007@nscss.com
http://www.nscss.org

Contact the NRCS for information on government soil conservation careers. Its Web site has information on volunteer opportunities.
Natural Resources Conservation Service (NRCS)
U.S. Department of Agriculture
Attn: Legislative and Public Affairs Division
PO Box 2890
Washington, DC 20013-2890
http://www.nrcs.usda.gov

For information on soil conservation, college student chapters, and publications, contact
Soil and Water Conservation Society
945 SW Ankeny Road
Ankeny, IA 50023-9723
Tel: 515-289-2331
http://www.swcs.org

For the career brochure Soils Sustain Life, *contact*
Soil Science Society of America
677 South Segoe Road
Madison, WI 53711-1086
Tel: 608-273-8080
http://www.soils.org

Soil Scientists

OVERVIEW

Soil scientists study the physical, chemical, and biological characteristics of soils to determine the most productive and effective planting strategies. Their research aids in producing larger, healthier crops and more environmentally sound farming procedures. There are about 30,000 agricultural and food scientists, a group that includes soil scientists, working in the United States.

HISTORY

Hundreds of years ago, farmers planted crops without restriction; they were unaware that soil could be depleted of necessary nutrients by overuse. When crops were poor, farmers often blamed the weather instead of their farming techniques.

Soil, one of our most important natural resources, was taken for granted until its condition became too bad to ignore. An increasing population, moreover, made the United States aware that its own welfare depends on fertile soil capable of producing food for hundreds of millions of people.

Increasing concerns about feeding a growing nation brought agricultural practices into reevaluation. In 1862, the U.S. Department of Agriculture (USDA) was created to give farmers information about new crops and improved farming techniques. Although the department started small, today the USDA is one of the largest agencies of the federal government.

Following the creation of the USDA, laws were created to further promote and protect farmers. The 1933 Agricultural Adjustment Act inaugurated a policy of giving direct government aid to farmers. Two years later, the Natural Resources Conservation Service developed after disastrous dust storms blew away millions of tons of valuable topsoil and destroyed fertile cropland throughout the Midwestern states.

Since 1937, states have organized themselves into soil conservation districts. Each local division coordinates with the USDA, assigning soil scientists and soil conservationists to help local farmers establish and maintain farming practices that will use land in the wisest possible ways.

THE JOB

Soil is formed by the breaking of rocks and the decay of trees, plants, and animals. It may take as long as 500 years to make just one inch of topsoil. Unwise and wasteful farming methods can destroy that inch of soil in just a few short years. In addition, rainstorms may carry thousands of pounds of precious topsoil away and dissolve chemicals that are necessary to grow healthy crops through a process called erosion. Soil scientists work with engineers to address these issues.

Soil scientists spend much of their time outdoors, investigating fields, advising farmers about crop rotation or fertilizers, assessing field drainage, and taking soil samples. After researching an area, they may suggest certain crops to farmers to protect bare earth from the ravages of the wind and weather.

Soil scientists may also specialize in one particular aspect of the work. For example, they may work as a *soil mapper* or *soil surveyor*. These specialists study soil structure, origins, and capabilities through field observations, laboratory examinations, and controlled experimentation. Their investigations are aimed at determining the most suitable uses for a particular soil.

Soil fertility experts develop practices that will increase or maintain crop size. They must consider both the type of soil and the crop planted in their analysis. Various soils react differently when exposed to fertilizers, soil additives, crop rotation, and other farming techniques.

All soil scientists work in the laboratory. They examine soil samples under the microscope to determine bacterial and plant-food components. They also write reports based on their field notes and analyses done within the lab.

Soil science is part of the science of agronomy, which encompasses crop science. Soil and crop scientists work together in agricultural experiment stations during all seasons, doing research on crop production, soil fertility, and various kinds of soil management.

A soil scientist (right) and an intern identify plant species for an inventory on Native Alaska lands near Homer, Alaska. *(Ron Nichols, Natural Resources Conservation Service)*

Some soil and crop scientists travel to remote sections of the world in search of plants and grasses that may thrive in this country and contribute to our food supply, pasture land, or soil replenishing efforts. Some scientists go overseas to advise farmers in other countries on how to treat their soils. Those with advanced degrees can teach college agriculture courses and conduct research projects.

REQUIREMENTS

High School

If you're interested in pursuing a career in agronomy, you should take college preparatory courses covering subjects such as math, science, English, and public speaking. Science courses, such as earth science, biology, and chemistry, are particularly important. Since much of your future work will involve calculations, you should take four years of high school math. You can learn a lot about farming methods and conditions by taking agriculture classes if your high school offers them. Computer science courses are also a good choice to familiarize yourself with this technology. You should also take English and speech courses, since soil scientists must write reports and make presentations about their findings.

Postsecondary Training

A bachelor's degree in agriculture or soil science is the minimum educational requirement to become a soil scientist. Typical courses include physics, geology, bacteriology, botany, chemistry, soil and plant morphology, soil fertility, soil classification, and soil genesis.

Research and teaching positions usually require higher levels of education. Most colleges of agriculture also offer master's and doctoral degrees. In addition to studying agriculture or soil science, students can specialize in biology, chemistry, physics, or engineering.

Certification or Licensing

Though not required, many soil scientists may seek certification to enhance their careers. The American Society of Agronomy offers certification programs in the following areas: crop advisory, agronomy, and soil science/classification. In order to be accepted into a program, applicants must meet certain levels of education and experience.

Other Requirements

Soil scientists must be able to work effectively both on their own and with others on projects, either outdoors or in the lab. Technology is increasingly used in this profession; an understanding of word processing, the Internet, multimedia software, databases, and even computer programming can be useful. Soil scientists spend many hours outdoors in all kinds of weather, so they must be able to endure sometimes difficult and uncomfortable physical conditions. They must be detail-oriented to do accurate research, and they should enjoy solving puzzles—figuring out, for example, why a crop isn't flourishing and what fertilizers should be used.

EXPLORING

The National FFA Organization can introduce you to the concerns of farmers and researchers. A 4-H club can also give you valuable

Earnings for Soil and Plant Scientists by Specialty, 2006

Industry	Mean Annual Earnings
Chemical and allied products merchants wholesalers	$83,620
Federal government	$67,530
Management of companies and enterprises	$66,070
Scientific research and development services	$63,790
Management, scientific, and technical consulting services	$49,530
Colleges, universities, and professional schools	$48,050

Source: U.S. Department of Labor

experience in agriculture. Contact the local branch of these organizations, your county's soil conservation department, or other government agencies to learn about regional projects. If you live in an agricultural community, you may be able to find opportunities for part-time or summer work on a farm or ranch.

EMPLOYERS

About 30,000 agricultural and food scientists, a group that includes soil scientists, work in the United States. Most soil scientists work for state or federal departments of agriculture. However, they may also work for other public employers, such as land appraisal boards, land-grant colleges and universities, and conservation departments. Soil scientists who work overseas may be employed by the U.S. Agency for International Development.

Soil scientists are needed in private industries as well, such as agricultural service companies, banks, insurance and real estate firms, food products companies, wholesale distributors, and environmental and engineering consulting groups. Private firms may hire soil scientists for sales or research positions.

STARTING OUT

In the public sector, college graduates can apply directly to the Natural Resources Conservation Service of the Department of Agriculture, the Department of the Interior, the Environmental Protection

Agency, or other state government agencies for beginning positions. University career services offices generally have listings for these openings as well as opportunities available in private industry.

ADVANCEMENT

Salary increases are the most common form of advancement for soil scientists. The nature of the job may not change appreciably even after many years of service. Higher administrative and supervisory positions are few in comparison with the number of jobs that must be done in the field.

Opportunities for advancement will be higher for those with advanced degrees. For soil scientists engaged in teaching, advancement may translate into a higher academic rank with more responsibility. In private business firms, soil scientists have opportunities to advance into positions such as department head or research director. Supervisory and manager positions are also available in state agencies such as road or conservation departments.

EARNINGS

According to the U.S. Department of Labor, median earnings in 2006 for soil and plant scientists were $56,080. The lowest paid 10 percent earned less than $33,650; the middle 50 percent earned between $42,410 and $72,020; and the highest paid 10 percent made more than $93,460.

Federal salaries for soil scientists were higher; in 2006, they made an average of $67,530 a year. Government earnings depend in large part on levels of experience and education. Those with doctorates and a great deal of experience may be qualified for higher government positions, with salaries ranging from $80,000 to $100,000. Other than short-term research projects, most jobs offer health and retirement benefits in addition to an annual salary.

WORK ENVIRONMENT

Most soil scientists work 40 hours a week. Their job is varied, ranging from fieldwork collecting samples, to labwork analyzing their findings. Some jobs may involve travel, even to foreign countries. Other positions may include teaching or supervisory responsibilities for field training programs.

OUTLOOK

The *Occupational Outlook Handbook* reports that employment within the field of soil science is expected to grow more slowly than the average for all occupations through 2014. The career of soil scientist is affected by the government's involvement in farming studies; as a result, budget cuts at the federal and (especially) state levels will limit funding for this type of job. However, private businesses will continue to demand soil scientists for research and sales positions. Companies dealing with seed, fertilizers, or farm equipment are examples of private industries that hire soil scientists.

Technological advances in equipment and methods of conservation will allow scientists to better protect the environment, as well as improve farm production. Scientists' ability to evaluate soils and plants will improve with more precise research methods. Combine-mounted yield monitors will produce data as the farmer crosses the field, and satellites will provide more detailed field information. With computer images, scientists will also be able to examine plant roots more carefully.

A continued challenge facing future soil scientists will be convincing farmers to change their current methods of tilling and chemical treatment in favor of environmentally safer methods. They must encourage farmers to balance increased agricultural output with the protection of our limited natural resources.

FOR MORE INFORMATION

The ASA has information on careers, certification, and college chapters.

American Society of Agronomy (ASA)
677 South Segoe Road
Madison, WI 53711-1086
Tel: 608-273-8080
Email: headquarters@agronomy.org
http://www.agronomy.org

Contact the NRCS for information on government soil conservation careers. Its Web site has information on volunteer opportunities.

Natural Resources Conservation Service (NRCS)
U.S. Department of Agriculture
Attn: Legislative and Public Affairs Division

PO Box 2890
Washington, DC 20013-2890
http://www.nrcs.usda.gov

For information on seminars, issues affecting soil scientists, and educational institutions offering soil science programs, contact
National Society of Consulting Soil Scientists
PO Box 1724
Sandpoint, ID 83864-0901
Tel: 800-535-7148
Email: info2007@nscss.com
http://www.nscss.org

For information on soil conservation, college student chapters, and publications, contact
Soil and Water Conservation Society
945 SW Ankeny Road
Ankeny, IA 50023-9723
Tel: 515-289-2331
http://www.swcs.org

For the career brochure Soils Sustain Life, *contact*
Soil Science Society of America
677 South Segoe Road
Madison, WI 53711-1086
Tel: 608-273-8080
http://www.soils.org

Writers, Horticulture

OVERVIEW

Writers express, edit, promote, and interpret ideas and facts in written form for books, magazines, trade journals, newspapers, technical studies and reports, company newsletters, radio and television broadcasts, and advertisements. Some writers specialize in a particular field, such as horticulture. These professionals write stories about a wide range of topics related to horticulture, such as a new public garden that has been created in a major city, the controversy over bioengineered crops, the growing popularity of eco-friendly horticultural techniques, and countless other topics. There are approximately 142,000 salaried writers and authors employed in the United States. Only a small percentage of this number specialize in writing about horticulture.

HISTORY

The skill of writing has existed for thousands of years. Egyptian papyrus fragments from 3000 B.C., and Chinese books dating back to 1300 B.C. are some examples of early writing. During the Middle Ages, books—mostly religious in theme—were copied and illustrated by hand. The development of the printing press by Johannes Gutenberg in the middle of the 15th century and the liberalism of the Protestant Reformation, which helped encourage a wider range of publications, greater literacy, and the creation of a number of works of literary merit, helped develop the publishing industry. The first authors worked directly with printers.

The modern publishing age began in the 18th century. Printing became mechanized, and the novel, magazine, and newspaper developed.

QUICK FACTS

School Subjects
Earth science
English
Journalism

Personal Skills
Communication/ideas
Helping/teaching

Work Environment
Indoors and outdoors
Primarily multiple locations

Minimum Education Level
Bachelor's degree

Salary Range
$25,430 to $48,640 to
$97,700+

Certification or Licensing
None available

Outlook
About as fast as the average

DOT
131

GOE
01.01.02

NOC
5121

O*NET-SOC
27-3043.00

In the late 1800s and early 1900s, large newspapers established sections devoted to horticulture, and magazines, such as *Better Homes & Gardens* (which was founded in 1922), targeted the public's interest in gardening.

Industry journals such as the *Journal of the American Society for Horticultural Science, Tree Care Industry,* and *Landscape Architecture* have also been created to present new ideas, techniques, and advances to horticulture professionals. Many horticulture writers also contribute to online counterparts of print journals, newspapers, and magazines.

In addition to the print media, the broadcasting industry has contributed to the development of the professional horticulture writer. Radio, television, and the Internet are sources of information, education, and entertainment that provide employment for many writers including those specializing in horticulture.

THE JOB

Writers work in the field of communications. Specifically, they deal with the written word, whether it is destined for the printed page, broadcast, or computer screen. The nature of their work is as varied as the materials they produce: books, magazines, trade journals, newspapers, technical reports, company newsletters and other publications, advertisements, speeches, and scripts for radio and television broadcast. Writers develop ideas and write for all media.

Writers, reporters, columnists, or critics working for horticulture-themed newspaper, magazine, and book publishers share many of the same duties. First they come up with an idea for an article or book from their own interests or are assigned a topic by an editor. A reporter specializing in horticulture, for example, could be assigned to write an article on methods to control Japanese beetles, which can cause significant damage to trees and plants. Then writers begin gathering as much information as possible about the subject through library research, interviews with horticultural scientists and perhaps homeowners with gardens affected by the beetles, the Internet, observation, and other methods. They keep extensive notes from which they will draw material for their project. Once the material has been organized and arranged in logical sequence, writers prepare a written outline. The process of developing a piece of writing is exciting, although it can also involve detailed and solitary work. After researching an idea, a writer might discover that a different perspective or related topic (for example, expanding the article to cover other garden pests—such as aphids, cabbage worm, cicadas, cucumber beetles, spider mites, and squash bugs) would be more effective, entertaining, or marketable.

When working on assignment, writers submit their outlines to an editor or other company representative for approval. Then they write a first draft of the manuscript, trying to put the material into words that will have the desired effect on their audience. They often rewrite or polish sections of the material as they proceed, always searching for just the right way of imparting information or expressing an idea or opinion. A manuscript may be reviewed, corrected, and revised numerous times before a final copy is submitted. Even after that, an editor may request additional changes.

Writers have a strong background in their specialty. For example, many horticulture writers have degrees in horticulture or a related subject, which provides them with a good background to write about the field. Some horticulture writers might be working horticultural scientists, landscape architects, farmers, or grounds managers. Horticulture writers may write weekly columns in the Home & Garden section of a newspaper, or submit stories to a magazine, such as *Organic Gardening,* that specializes in a horticulture-related topic. Horticulture writers may also relay complicated scientific information into material easily understood by the general public in books, newsletters, magazines, or newspaper articles. Association trade publications, such as *HortTechnology* (which is published by the American Society for Horticultural Science), may have writers on staff or use articles written by freelancers. Some horticulture writers may be assigned to write scholarly material such as school textbooks or industry journals.

Some horticulture writers may teach others about writing at colleges and universities or in local community writing groups. Others may become experts in the field and give talks about horticulture at arboretums, nature museums, and in other settings.

REQUIREMENTS
High School
While in high school, build a broad educational foundation by taking courses in English, literature, foreign languages, history, general science, social studies, computer science, and typing. The ability to type is almost a requisite for all positions in the communications field, as is familiarity with computers. Classes in earth science, horticulture, and agriculture will also be very useful.

Postsecondary Training

Competition for writing jobs almost always demands the background of a college education. Many employers prefer you have a broad liberal arts background or majors in English, literature, history, philosophy, or one of the social sciences. Other employers desire communications or journalism training in college. If you plan on specializing in horticulture, you should earn a degree, or at least minor, in horticulture or in the particular horticulture specialty (agriculture, botany, landscape architecture, soil science, etc.) that you would like to pursue. Occasionally a master's degree in a specialized writing field may be required. A number of schools offer courses in journalism, and some of them offer courses or majors in book publishing, publication management, and newspaper and magazine writing.

In addition to formal course work, most employers look for practical writing experience. If you have worked on high school or college newspapers, yearbooks, or literary magazines, you will make a better candidate, as well as if you have worked for small community newspapers or radio stations, even in an unpaid position. Many book publishers, magazines, newspapers, and radio and television stations have summer internship programs that provide valuable training if you want to learn about the publishing and broadcasting businesses. Interns do many simple tasks, such as running errands and answering phones, but some may be asked to perform research, conduct interviews, or even write some minor pieces.

Other Requirements

To be a writer, you should be creative and able to express ideas clearly, have a broad general knowledge, be skilled in research techniques, and be computer literate. You should also have a keen interest in horticulture and related fields. Other assets include curiosity, persistence, initiative, resourcefulness, and an accurate memory. For some jobs—on a newspaper, for example, where the activity is hectic and deadlines are short—the ability to concentrate and produce under pressure is essential.

EXPLORING

As a high school or college student, you can test your interest and aptitude in the field of writing by serving as a reporter or writer on school newspapers, yearbooks, and literary magazines. Various writing courses and workshops will offer you the opportunity to sharpen your writing skills. Of course, writing about horticulture-related topics as much as possible is one of the best ways to try out the field and build your writing skills.

Small community newspapers and local magazines or trade publications often welcome contributions from outside sources, although they may not have the resources to pay for them. Jobs in bookstores, magazine shops, and even newsstands will offer you a chance to become familiar with various publications.

You can also obtain information on writing as a career by visiting local newspapers, industry trade magazines, publishers, or radio and television stations and interviewing some of the writers who work there. Career conferences and other guidance programs frequently include speakers on the entire field of communications from local or national organizations.

EMPLOYERS

There are approximately 142,000 writers and authors currently employed in the United States, but only a small percentage of writers specialize in horticulture. Nearly 50 percent of salaried writers and editors work for newspaper, periodical, book, and directory publishers; radio and television broadcasting; software publishers; motion picture and sound-recording industries; Internet service providers, Web search portals, and data-processing services; and Internet publishing and broadcasting, according to the *Occupational Outlook Handbook*. Writers are also employed by advertising agencies and public relations firms, and for journals and newsletters published by business and nonprofit organizations, such as professional associations, labor unions, and religious organizations. Other employers are government agencies.

STARTING OUT

A fair amount of experience is required to gain a high-level position in the field. Most horticulture writers start out in entry-level positions. These jobs may be listed with college career services offices, or they may be obtained by applying directly to the employment departments of the individual publishers or broadcasting companies. Graduates who previously served internships with these companies often have the advantage of knowing someone who can give them a personal recommendation. Want ads in newspapers and trade journals are another source for jobs. Because of the competition for positions, however, few vacancies are listed with public or private employment agencies.

Employers in the communications field usually are interested in samples of published writing. These are often assembled in an organized portfolio or scrapbook. Bylined or signed articles are more credible (and, as a result, more useful) than stories whose source is not identified.

Beginning positions as a junior writer usually involve library research, preparation of rough drafts for part or all of a report, cataloging, and other related writing tasks. These are generally carried on under the supervision of a senior writer.

ADVANCEMENT

Most writers find their first jobs as editorial or production assistants. Advancement may be more rapid in small companies, where beginners learn by doing a little bit of everything and may be given writing tasks immediately. In large firms, duties are usually more compartmentalized. Assistants in entry-level positions are assigned such tasks as research, fact checking, and copyrighting, but it generally takes much longer to advance to full-scale writing duties.

Promotion into more responsible positions may come with the assignment of more important articles and stories to write, or it may be the result of moving to another company. Mobility among employees in this field is common. An assistant in one publishing house may switch to an executive position in another. Or a writer may switch to a related field as a type of advancement.

Freelance or self-employed writers earn advancement in the form of larger fees as they gain exposure and establish their reputations.

EARNINGS

In 2006, median annual earnings for salaried writers and authors were $48,640 a year, according to the U.S. Department of Labor. The lowest paid 10 percent earned less than $25,430, while the highest paid 10 percent earned $97,700 or more. Writers who were employed by newspaper, periodical, and book publishers earned mean annual salaries of $47,140 in 2006.

In addition to their salaries, many horticulture writers earn some income from freelance work. Part-time freelancers may earn from $5,000 to $15,000 a year. Freelance earnings vary widely. Full-time established freelance writers may earn more than $75,000 a year.

WORK ENVIRONMENT

Working conditions vary for horticulture writers. Although their workweek usually runs 35 to 40 hours, many writers work overtime. A publication that is issued frequently has more deadlines closer together, creating greater pressures to meet them. The work is especially hectic on newspapers, which operate seven days a week. Writers often work nights and weekends to meet deadlines or to cover a late-developing story.

Most writers work independently, but they often must cooperate with graphic designers, photographers, rewriters, and advertising people who may have widely differing ideas of how the materials should be prepared and presented.

Physical surroundings range from comfortable private offices to noisy, crowded newsrooms filled with other workers typing and talking on the telephone. Some horticulture writers must confine their research to the library or telephone interviews, but others may travel to other cities or countries or to local sites, such as gardens, parks, forests, prairies, farms, golf courses, vineyards, garden centers, nurseries, research laboratories, and other locations.

The work is arduous, but most horticulture writers are seldom bored. Some jobs require travel. The most difficult element is the continual pressure of deadlines. People who are the most content as writers enjoy and work well with deadline pressure.

OUTLOOK

The employment of all writers is expected to increase about as fast as the average for all occupations through 2014, according to the U.S. Department of Labor. The demand for writers by newspapers, periodicals, book publishers, and trade associations is expected to increase. The growth of online publishing on company Web sites and other online services will also demand many talented writers; those with computer skills will be at an advantage as a result.

The American public is increasingly interested in learning more about gardening and horticulture. In fact, there were 174 magazines alone in 2006 that specialized in gardening and horticulture (a nearly 15 percent increase from 2004), according to the *National Directory of Magazines*. And newspapers are also creating new print and online gardening sections to attract readers. As a result, opportunities should be good for well-qualified horticulture writers.

People entering this field should realize that the competition for jobs is extremely keen. Beginners, especially, may have difficulty finding employment. Of the thousands who graduate each year with degrees in English, journalism, communications, and the liberal arts, intending to establish a career as a writer, many turn to other occupations when they find that applicants far outnumber the job openings available. College students would do well to keep this in mind and prepare for an unrelated alternate career in the event they are unable to obtain a position as writer; another benefit of this approach is that, at the same time, they will become qualified as writers in a specialized field. The practicality of preparing for alternate careers is borne out by the fact that opportunities are best in firms that prepare business and trade publications and in technical writing.

FOR MORE INFORMATION

For information on careers, gardening trends, and membership, contact
Garden Writers Association
10210 Leatherleaf Court
Manassas, VA 20111
Tel: 703-257-1032
http://www.gwaa.org

The MPA is a good source of information about internships.
Magazine Publishers of America (MPA)
810 Seventh Avenue, 24th Floor
New York, NY 10019-5873
Tel: 212-872-3700
Email: mpa@magazine.org
http://www.magazine.org

For information about working as a writer and union membership, contact
National Writers Union
113 University Place, 6th Floor
New York, NY 10003-4527
Tel: 212-254-0279
Email: nwu@nwu.org
http://www.nwu.org

This organization for journalists has campus and online chapters.
Society of Professional Journalists
Eugene S. Pulliam National Journalism Center
3909 North Meridian Street
Indianapolis, IN 46208-4011
Tel: 317-927-8000
http://www.spj.org

Index